THE COMFORTER: THE SPIRIT OF JOY

✝

To Huguette,

    May the Comforter fill you with His special love, joy and peace!

        Fr. Andrew

THE COMFORTER:
The Spirit of Joy

ANDREW APOSTOLI, CFR

ALBA·HOUSE   NEW·YORK

SOCIETY OF ST. PAUL, 2187 VICTORY BLVD., STATEN ISLAND, NEW YORK 10314

Library of Congress Cataloging-in-Publication Data

Apostoli, Andrew.
    The Comforter: the Spirit of joy / Andrew Apostoli.
        p.   cm.
    ISBN 0-8189-0734-7
    1. Holy Spirit. 2. Joy — Religious aspects — Christianity.
    3. Spiritual life — Catholic Church. 4. Catholic Church — Doctrines.
    I. Title.
    BT121.2.A65   1995
    231'.3 — dc20   95-3954
                                                  CIP

Produced and designed in the United States of America by the
Fathers and Brothers of the Society of St. Paul,
2187 Victory Boulevard, Staten Island, New York 10314,
as part of their communications apostolate.

ISBN: 0-8189-0734-7

Printing Information:

Current Printing - first digit   2   3   4   5   6   7   8   9   10

Year of Current Printing - first year shown

                                                      1999   2000

Dedication

This book is lovingly dedicated to
the Blessed Virgin Mary, the Cause of Our Joy.

As the instrument of the Holy Spirit,
she willingly shared the joys and sorrows of her divine Son, Jesus,
as He accomplished the Father's will faithfully
in His life and in His death.

May she intercede for us to share also
in the joys and sorrows of her Son here on earth
so that some day we may share
in the fullness of His joy and glory
in the kingdom of Heaven.

Acknowledgments

I wish to acknowledge the generous help of a number of persons who assisted in the making of this book. Special thanks go to three individuals. First to His Eminence, John Cardinal O'Connor who, despite the many demands on his time, graciously agreed to write the Foreword for this book. Second to Mary Majkowski who faithfully and generously typed the text. (Also special thanks are extended to her family for their kindness to me on many occasions when I visited with them to work on the book.) Third to Renee Bumb for her kindness in editing the text to prepare it for publication.

I would also like to thank all those who offered assistance and encouragement as this book was in preparation, especially for those who supported this project in prayer. I would also like to thank Sister Helen Sanchez, M.P.F., for her helpful suggestions. The author also would like to thank Alba House for kindly agreeing to publish this work.

No acknowledgment would be complete without thanking Almighty God from Whom all blessings flow. May this book redound to the glory and praise of the Most Holy Trinity. I wish to express special thanks to Our Blessed Lady whose joy was an inspiration during the writing of this book. Finally, I wish to acknowledge the intercession of St. Therese of Lisieux (who knew the trials of an author as she wrote her own *Story of a Soul*), as well as the Servants of God, Padre Pio of Pietrelcina, O.F.M. Cap. and Fr. Solanus Casey, O.F.M. Cap. whose prayerful support was daily sought throughout the preparation of this book.

Table of Contents

Foreword

"Great joy has in it the sense of immortality," said G.K. Chesterton in *Heresies*; "the very splendor of youth is that it has all space to stretch its legs in."

It is time for a book on joy, and past time. While there is haunting beauty, indeed, in Gerard Manley Hopkins' having the Holy Spirit *brood* over a bent world, I like Father Andrew's emphasis on the same Holy Spirit as Comforter. And I am especially taken by his gentle insights into Our Lady's role as Cause of Our Joy.

Saint Thérèse of Lisieux is treated here appropriately in a section on the suffering of saints, as is Saint Francis. Father Andrew's labors will be well rewarded if readers come to understand that neither is a mere "holy card" saint, as each is too frequently portrayed. Suffering was of the warp and woof of their lives, but each breathed joy.

The rootedness of the joy of the Holy Spirit in love, of course, has to be viewed as the heart of this welcome work. Nor would anyone who knows Father Andrew personally be surprised that such is the case. His own love for the poor radiates in all he says, in all he does. He is truly, in the Holy Spirit, their comforter. He is but a vessel, as he knows so very well; indeed, because he knows it so well, he is completely open to the very joy of the Spirit that uses him to rejoice others.

I will be particularly happy to have this book on my night stand. It is often in the darkest hours of the night that one needs the comfort of the Holy Spirit, the Spirit of Joy.

John Cardinal O'Connor

Introduction

This is my second book dealing with the Holy Spirit. The first, *The Gift of God: the Holy Spirit* (Alba House, 1994), focused on Who the Holy Spirit is. It dealt with Him as the foremost "Gift of God," promised by our Heavenly Father and sent to us as part of Jesus' glorification to continue Jesus' work on earth and bring us the fullness of God's gifts and graces. It likewise dealt with the Holy Spirit as the source of our spiritual life, with a special emphasis on the courage He gives us to persevere in loving and serving Jesus faithfully, even in the face of great trials and considerable opposition.

This present book emphasizes the Holy Spirit's role of bringing forth His fruit of joy in our Christian lives. It is a unique joy, one the world cannot give because it does not know Jesus.

This book contains two main sections.

The first section deals with the Holy Spirit as the Comforter, Who enables us to taste the sweetness of the things of God. In this way, He draws us ever more deeply into a living relationship with the Father in, through, and with Jesus. Anyone who has tasted this "sweetness of the Lord" knows the unspeakable joy and delight of the Comforter.

The second section deals with the spiritual growth of a Christian from the status of a beginner to that of full maturity. Using the experience of the Apostles as our guide (and after all, who had a better Spiritual Director than they did?), it traces this spiritual growth through various stages. As we will see, these stages are related to an increasing understanding of the wisdom, power and even joy flowing from the Cross of the Savior. All this hits at the heart of that great Christian paradox, namely, that in this life, sorrow and joy are intermingled! It was this way for Jesus, for Our Lady, for the Apostles, for the saints. It will be the same for all those who generously choose to follow the path of Christian holiness. The Holy Spirit, the Comforter, leads us into the heart of this paradox where alone we will find the joy and peace for which our hearts were made and our spirits yearn.

In life we all need to gain insights into ourselves so that we can be challenged to grow and to become all that God has called us to be. Many times these insights come from our friends; occasionally, however, they come even from our enemies. One such "enemy" of God and the Church was the philosopher, Friedrich Nietzsche, one of the fathers of modern atheism (famous for his saying, "God is dead"). He put a couple of challenges before Christians of our day. One was his remark: "If you want me to believe in a Redeemer, why don't you look a little more redeemed?" Certainly he has a valid point: hypocrisy — preaching one thing but doing another — is a real detriment and stumbling block for non-believers to come to believe.

But it is really to a second challenge from Nietzsche that I want to refer. He is quoted as saying: "The reason people no longer believe (in God) is because believers (in God) no longer sing!" This is a more subtle criticism — but a very valuable one for the mission of the Church. His challenge is this: when people are very happy, they spontaneously break into song and, as the expression goes, they sometimes "sing their hearts out." What Nietzsche is saying is that so many today who claim to believe in God and love Him — factors which should certainly fill them with supreme joy — do not "sing": they show no happiness in their Christian lives! Their practice of the Faith seems so routine, so boring, so lifeless. Their enthusiasm in the Lord no longer bubbles over into spontaneous joy! Something is missing, he is saying, on the part of many believers to want to make others become believers, too.

In contrast, when joy is evident, it cannot be hidden. St. Francis is a saint known for his joy in loving God. And he was a singer, too! Sometimes he would pick up two sticks; one he would use like a fiddle, and the other he would use like a bow. Then, making his own music, he would share his joy with others. Another example was his writing of a canticle or hymn in praise of God for all His creatures. It is called the Canticle of the Creatures. He wanted to give expression to the beauty and harmony of all creation in praising God, so much so that he related in a unique way to all God's creatures, calling them "brother sun" and "sister moon," "brother wind," "sister water" and "brother fire."

But most telling of all was an incident that occurred shortly after St. Francis' conversion to the Lord. He was walking in a woods not far from his beloved little chapel of St. Mary of the Angels. He was imitating the troubadours who, as poet-musicians, would go about singing ballads about the chivalry and love stories of the knights. This troubadour of Christ was singing out his praises of God and his great love for the One Who had loved him so much. All of a sudden, three thieves came upon the little poor man of Assisi. They asked him: "Who are you?" St. Francis answered: "I am the herald of the Great King!" Seeing his poor clothing and humble appearance the thieves laughed him to scorn. They threw him into the mud and snow then covering the ground. "Lay there, you herald of the Great King," they said in mocking tones. And off they went, laughing. What did St. Francis do? He got up, dusted himself off, and undaunted he began to pour out his heart again in joyful song, filling the woods with the praises and love of God. His was the song of an enthusiastic and joyous believer which has continued to be heard (in the power of his example) for more than 800 years. And it has made believers of many!

The Church, to be seen as authentic, must radiate the message of the Gospel with the power of joy in the lives of those who claim to know, love and serve Jesus! It must be the Holy Spirit

Who gives us this joy. We need the Comforter to teach us how to "sing" out our love and praise of God.

In our own times, another saintly person has shown us the profound power of joy in proclaiming the Christian message. This is Mother Teresa of Calcutta. The spirit of her Missionaries of Charity is summed up in three important qualities: loving trust, total surrender, and boundless good cheer. Mother Teresa knows well the power of cheerfulness or joy. She tells her Sisters that a cheerful Sister preaches without preaching: "Joy speaks for itself." And she adds: "A cheerful Sister is like a net which catches souls for God." Whereas a cold or hard or overly serious demeanor scares people away, cheerfulness or joy attracts them like bees to honey. As St. Francis de Sales, a rather joyous saint himself, would say: "You will attract more bees with an ounce of honey than a barrel of vinegar."

Our age has been characterized by profound human suffering. World wars and wars of ethnic cleansing, persecutions and concentration camps, famine, plague and natural disasters of all kinds have characterized our 20th century. Add to these many personal and family trials as well as the overall negative effects of the materialism and secularism of our times, and we can see clearly why life has come to seem so purposeless, pessimistic and even fatalistic to many. Despite all the technical advances of our times, a real lack of joy and satisfaction abounds. There is an emptiness and pain in the hearts and souls of so many people today. Yet, like a brilliant light dispelling the darkness, the Holy Spirit brings us a joy that gives meaning and enthusiasm to life, and comfort and strength in the face of its difficulties.

It is my fervent hope and prayer that all those who read this book may experience an increase of the surpassing joy and consolation the Comforter brings to those who seek Jesus. In turn, I ask a kind remembrance in prayer.

Fr. Andrew Apostoli, C.F.R.

CHAPTER I

The Comforter

O UR LORD, IN HIS FAREWELL discourse, frequently referred to the Holy Spirit as the Paraclete (John chs. 14-16). In ancient Greece the word "paraclete" meant a lawyer or, more literally, "someone who stands at the side of another" to defend and encourage. In reference to the Holy Spirit, therefore, "Paraclete" is frequently rendered "Advocate." Sometimes, however, it is also rendered as "Comforter" or "Consoler." This is because we attribute to the Holy Spirit, in a special way, the role of filling us with spiritual joy and consolation. This role is reflected in the inspiring Sequence for the Mass of Pentecost, the "Veni, Sancte Spiritus" ("Come, Holy Spirit").

> You, of Comforters the best;
> You, the soul's most welcome Guest;
> Sweet refreshment here below.
>
> In our labor, rest most sweet;
> Grateful coolness in the heat;
> Solace in the midst of woe.

THE JOY COMING FROM THE HOLY SPIRIT

The Sacred Scriptures abundantly prove that the Holy Spirit is a special source of joy in the Christian life. The experience of the saints as well as our own confirm this belief. I once saw a poster with

1

the message: "Joy is the most infallible sign of the presence of God." How true these words are! When God is present in us by Sanctifying Grace, we experience a certain joy and peace that is not experienced when He is absent from the soul. This is because joy is a fruit of the Holy Spirit living and working within us.

JOY: FRUIT OF THE HOLY SPIRIT

St. Paul stresses this point. When he lists the main fruits of the Holy Spirit, he mentions joy as the second of them:

> The fruit of the Spirit is love, joy, peace, patient endurance, kindness, generosity, faith, mildness and chastity (Galatians 5:22-23).

Understandably, St. Paul places love as the first fruit of the Holy Spirit. This is because God's very being is love (1 John 4:8, 16), and so He produces love in us as the first of His fruits because it is the very likeness of Himself. But from love springs joy. It is therefore logical that joy should follow love, for everyone who truly loves finds joy with the persons they love. They also find joy in serving them. Far from being a burden, the opportunity to serve gives great satisfaction and happiness.

Further, St. Paul lists joy just ahead of peace as a fruit of the Holy Spirit because peace is the fulfillment and completion of love and joy. Peace is joy possessed more fully and permanently; when joy satisfies the longing of the heart, then the heart is at peace.

At the Last Supper, Our Lord promised to give His Apostles both His joy (John 15:11) and His peace (John 14:27). He fulfilled these promises on Easter night when His risen presence made them rejoice exceedingly (John 20:20; Luke 24:41) and He greeted them with His peace (John 20:21). It is not a mere coincidence that this was also the same occasion when He bestowed upon them a special outpouring of the Holy Spirit Himself (John 20:22), Who would preserve this joy and peace within them.

JOY: ESSENTIAL ELEMENT OF THE KINGDOM

St. Paul again links joy as well as peace with the Holy Spirit. He described these fruits of the Spirit as essential characteristics of the Kingdom when he wrote to the Christians at Rome:

> The Kingdom of God is not a matter of eating and drinking, but of justice, peace and that joy that is given by the Holy Spirit (Romans 14:17).

Here the Apostle emphasizes that the happiness of the Kingdom of God is not of a sensual nature, like the pleasures found in eating and drinking which are often pagan concepts of happiness. Rather, it is the satisfaction found in mind and heart when they are filled with justice, peace, and joy. Justice, like love, orients us properly to God and our neighbor, by moving us to give them what is their due. From such justice comes the interior peace of a good conscience that rests confidently in God. Finally, there comes that joy which floods our souls when we possess the One we love and are in turn possessed by Him.

"Rejoice in the Lord Always!"

St. Paul expresses the conviction that joyfulness should characterize Christians in their daily living. It is not to be an exceptional or even occasional experience, but rather a continuous attitude of mind and heart. Here is how he stated the case to his beloved Philippians:

> Rejoice in the Lord always! I say it again: Rejoice! Everyone should see how unselfish you are. The Lord is near. Dismiss all anxiety from your minds. Present your needs to God in every form of prayer and in petitions full of gratitude. Then God's own peace, which is beyond all understanding, will stand guard over your hearts and minds, in Christ Jesus (Philippians 4:4-7).

This joy is not so much an emotional sensation, like a nice warm feeling or sensible consolation, but rather a ready disposition to do cheerfully whatever is asked of us. Such a joyful attitude can be present even when we are experiencing difficulties of all sorts. In fact, elsewhere St. Paul described himself and his co-workers as "sorrowful, though we are always rejoicing" (2 Corinthians 6:10).

St. Paul states that the secret of a distinctively Christian joy is the fact that "the Lord is near." The basis of all authentic joy from the Holy Spirit is the virtue of hope. It is the belief that God is always near us, and that He can and will help us in all circumstances. Therefore, we must "dismiss all anxiety" from our minds.

The Apostle further stresses that if the Lord is near, we can make known to Him all our needs in prayer, turning to Him with both confidence and gratitude. This brings about an unbelievable peace in our hearts and forms the basis of constant rejoicing in Jesus through the working of the Holy Spirit within us.

EXAMPLES OF JOY IN THE SCRIPTURES

The Sacred Scriptures provide many powerful examples of joyfulness. Let us begin with the examples in the lives of Our Lord and His Blessed Mother.

JOY IN THE LIFE OF JESUS

In regard to Our Lord, the Scriptures refer both to His constant attitude of joyfulness as well as to very specific moments of joy and consolation.

Jesus' Constant Attitude of Joyfulness

At the Last Supper, Our Lord referred to what He called "My joy." He told His Apostles that they would share His joy so that their own joy may be complete (John 15:11). Toward the end of the supper, He prayed to His Heavenly Father that His disciples "may share My joy completely" (John 17:13). Furthermore, Our Lord indicated that when the Apostles received joy from His Resurrection appearances and from His gifts, it would be a joy that no one else could ever take from them (John 16:16, 22). These statements clearly reveal that Our Lord possessed a fullness of joy. He would share this joy with His followers in many ways, but primarily through the work of the Holy Spirit.

The joy of God, like His Sanctifying Grace, is a gift that can only be lost through our own fault. He will never take it back from us on His own, nor can someone ever take it from us against our own will. But we can surrender it or lose it through sin. The reason is simple. Whenever we do God's will, even in adversity, we can still possess that attitude of inner joyfulness and peace. However, because sin is the selfish choosing of our own will over God's will, we lose His inner joy and peace to the degree we set our wills against His. In venial sin we lose these gifts more or less in the measure we offend God; in mortal sin we lose them altogether and need to regain them through repentance and confession.

In this light we can understand St. Paul's remarks about doing nothing to "sadden the Holy Spirit" (Ephesians 4:30). Because the Holy Spirit is God, He is infinitely joy-filled and therefore nothing we can do could ever possibly make Him sad. When we sin, however, we can and do experience guilt, remorse, and sadness in our own hearts, and this will affect the joy of the Spirit's presence in us. It is not really the Holy Spirit Who experiences sadness from our sins; we do.

Like the Apostles, we also can share in this gift of Our Lord's joy. It will provide us with a constant inner attitude of doing cheerfully whatever God asks of us. It makes it easier to resist temptations to sin against God's commandments. It can give us courage to make greater efforts in doing good for God's honor and glory and for the welfare of our neighbor. It can fill us with a generosity to make any sacrifices that we or others need. Our joy will be full because Jesus will share with us from the fullness of His own joy! This joy will remain alive and active in us through the power and presence of the Holy Spirit working within us. Like a tree laden with fruit at the harvest time, so the Holy Spirit will see that our hearts are filled abundantly with the fruit of joy He continuously brings forth in us.

Jesus Experiences Joyous Consolation in Prayer

Besides a continuous attitude of inner joyfulness, Our Lord also experienced the joy of the Holy Spirit in a special way on certain specific occasions. One such example was when the seventy-two disciples He had sent out to preach returned to Him from their missionary journey. They were enthusiastically reporting to Him all that they had done in His Name, even casting out demons. Our Lord took the occasion to warn them against pride and any false spiritual security that could result from the feeling that even the evil spirits were subject to them. He cautioned them:

> Do not rejoice so much in the fact that the devils are subject to you as that your names are inscribed in Heaven (Luke 10:20).

What Our Lord is saying is that the disciples' real joy comes from the hope of eternal life held out for them because their "names are inscribed in Heaven," and not from any exercise of power in His Name. What follows is a description of Our Lord Himself experiencing authentic joy in the Holy Spirit as He prayed to His Heavenly Father:

> At that moment Jesus rejoiced in the Holy Spirit and said: "I offer You praise, O Father, Lord of heaven and earth, because what You have hidden from the learned and the clever You have revealed to the merest children" (Luke 10:21).

The joy Our Lord experienced here through the influence of the Holy Spirit was an emotional sensation of joy, much like the sensible consolations the Holy Spirit also gives us, particularly during prayer. St. Luke gives us the precise reason for Our Lord's consolation: He rejoiced because His Heavenly Father was revealing His Wisdom to "the merest children." We can presume here that Our Lord means the seventy-two disciples, who for the most part were probably simple and unlearned, but deeply faith-filled. Our Lord sees His disciples maturing in wisdom, and this causes Him to experience a great joyous consolation. Like Our Lord, we, too, often experience the Holy Spirit's fruit of joy in moments of consolation in prayer. It is with good reason that we also call the Holy Spirit the "Consoler."

THE HOLY SPIRIT AND THE JOYS OF OUR LADY

We often associate a number of "joyful" events or "mysteries" with the life of our Blessed Mother. They are especially found in the first two chapters of St. Luke's Gospel. What joy must Our Lady have experienced at the Annunciation when the Holy Spirit overshadowed her and she conceived the Christ Child within her! Or, what joy there must have been at Bethlehem when Our Lady gave birth to the Christ Child, when even the angels described His birth to the shepherds that night as "good news. . . tidings of great joy to be shared by the whole people" (Luke 2:10)! Or again, what great joy must have been experienced by Our Lady and St. Joseph when, after searching "in sorrow" (Luke 2:48) for the Child Jesus for three days, they come across Him safe and sound in the Temple!

The Joy of the Visitation

The Visitation, however, most clearly expresses the joyfulness of Our Lady. She had come in haste to assist her aged cousin

Elizabeth, now six months pregnant with her son John. St. Luke describes the joyful encounter:

> Mary. . . entered Zechariah's house and greeted Elizabeth. When Elizabeth heard Mary's greeting, the baby leapt in her womb. Elizabeth was filled with the Holy Spirit and cried out in a loud voice: "Blest are you among women and blest is the fruit of your womb. But who am I that the mother of my Lord should come to me? The moment your greeting sounded in my ears, the baby leapt in my womb for joy. Blest is she who trusted that the Lord's words to her would be fulfilled" (Luke 1:40-45).

What untold joy filled this whole encounter! Our Lady, carrying the Christ Child within her womb, radiated the joy of Jesus' presence and His saving power to others. The Holy Spirit, Who had overshadowed Our Lady at her Annunciation, is now working in her as His chosen instrument to spread His consolation to others. Wherever Our Lady goes, God uses her to touch the lives of those around her.

Elizabeth, a woman of deep faith and openness to God's presence, receives the Holy Spirit at the moment of Our Lady's coming. Even though they are cousins, Elizabeth recognizes Our Lady's surpassing holiness and the divine favor she enjoys: "Who am I that the Mother of my Lord should come to me?" When Our Lady greeted her, Elizabeth was filled with such overwhelming joy that even the child in her womb leapt for joy!

Finally, Elizabeth recognizes under the Spirit's inspiration the reason for Our Lady's exalted mission: she "trusted that the Lord's words to her would be fulfilled." Our Lady's unwavering faith and trust in response to God's word at the Annunciation were absolutely essential to God's plan of salvation.

Now it is Our Lady's turn once again to rejoice. Under the Spirit's inspiration, she now breaks forth into her joyous canticle of praise and thanksgiving, her "Magnificat":

> My being proclaims the greatness of the Lord,
> My spirit finds joy in God my Savior
> For He has looked upon His servant in her lowliness;
> All ages to come shall call me blessed. . . (Luke 1:46-48).

In the most profound humility befitting the one who has been exalted over all other creatures, Our Lady praises God for His greatness and for all the wonderful things He has done for her. Our Lady's song is not one of pride; this would have been totally alien to one who called herself the "handmaid of the Lord" (Luke 1:38). Rather, it is a canticle acknowledging all the "great things" the mighty God has done for her. Finally, Our Lady reveals that her "spirit finds joy in God." We can not even begin to fathom the sweetness of the joy with which the Holy Spirit has filled the inner heart of Our Lady.

There are important lessons in the joy of Our Lady for all of us. We should ask her to be near us always so that we may experience the inner joyfulness she radiates, even in our times of trial and suffering. According to St. Bonaventure, we should also ask Our Lady to obtain for us gifts she herself possessed: souls that "proclaim the greatness of the Lord" and spirits that "find joy in God our Savior." With Our Lady as Mother and model, we can walk joyfully along the path of life, both in good times and in bad. Our Lady while on earth was the woman of the joyful mysteries as well as of the "sorrowful"; now in Heaven she is forever the woman of the "glorious mysteries." If we are faithful, the Holy Spirit will keep us close to her joys and sorrows as we journey on our pilgrimage of faith in this life so that in eternity we may share with her the endless glory of Her divine Son. How proper it is that we invoke Our Lady in her Litany as "Cause of Our Joy"!

THE ROLE OF THE COMFORTER IN THE EARLY CHURCH

Having looked at some examples of the joys of Jesus and Mary, we now focus more closely in the Scriptures on the Holy Spirit's role as "Comforter" in the days of the early Church.

There we find many examples of the Holy Spirit bringing comfort and consolation to the Apostles. This joy of the Holy Spirit sustained them in their spiritual growth and helped them to overcome the difficulties and opposition they encountered. There are, however, a few other references that tell us clearly of the work of the Comforter in the early Church.

The Holy Spirit poured forth His fruit of joy to support the mission of evangelization in the early Church. We read in Acts, for instance, that when the deacon Philip preached in Samaria his words as well as his miraculous healings and his exorcisms of evil spirits had a profound impact on the people. St. Luke sums up the people's reaction to Philip's ministry:

The rejoicing in that town rose to fever pitch (Acts 8:8).

Further on, St. Luke describes the effect of Philip's ministry on an Ethiopian court official. Philip had spoken to him about Jesus as the fulfillment of the Old Testament prophecies. The official then asked Philip to baptize him. When the baptism was concluded, the Holy Spirit "snatched Philip away." The official, for his part, "went on his way rejoicing" (Acts 8:39).

A final example of the joy given by the Holy Spirit to the Church is again recorded by St. Luke in Acts. He gives a summary of the general state of the Church following the stoning of St. Stephen and the violent persecution begun against the Christians by Saul of Tarsus. After the conversion of Saul, we find the Church enjoying a period of great peace and consolation from the Holy Spirit.

Meanwhile throughout all Judea, Galilee and Samaria the Church was at peace. It was being built up and was making steady progress in the fear of the Lord; at the same time it enjoyed the increased consolation of the Holy Spirit (Acts 9:31).

This peaceful comfort of the Holy Spirit proved only to be temporary because more frequent and more violent persecutions would lie ahead for the Church as her long history attests. But like a serene calm after one storm but before another, the Comforter increased His joy and consolation to the Church as she experienced an increase of the sorrows and the desolation of various trials and persecutions.

CHAPTER II

Our Own Need for the Comforter

WHAT THE HOLY SPIRIT HAS always done and still continues to do for the Church as a whole, He does for each
individual Christian. He brings us the fruit of His joy
in abundance. What are our needs for the joys and consolations of
the Holy Spirit? Let us reflect on some of them.

JOY LIGHTENS OUR BURDENS

Joy certainly lightens the burdens of daily life. Life's duties
have a way of getting us down. Under the weight of daily pressures
and responsibilities, life can easily become too serious. We can lose
our ability to laugh at ourselves. We start to exaggerate our
problems until we convince ourselves that we are carrying the
weight of the world upon our shoulders. We become distressed,
feeling upset with everything and everybody. As a result, we are
ready to jump out at people.

Joy lightens the situation. Joy makes us less inclined to brood
over things, to weigh each effort, to complain incessantly. We give
more readily when joy fills our hearts. Cheerfulness makes giving
and even sacrificing easier. St. Paul offered wise advice to the
Christians at Corinth about a cheerful spirit of giving. While taking
up a collection for the poor in Jerusalem, the Apostle instructed the
Corinthians that they have no obligation to give everything they
possessed (otherwise they would be poor), but rather, with a good

13

conscience they should each determine in the secrecy of their own hearts the amount to give. Above all, St. Paul emphasized that they give with a joyous attitude.

> Everyone must give according to what he has inwardly decided; not sadly, not grudgingly, for God loves a cheerful giver (2 Corinthians 9:7).

St. Paul warns us against giving sadly or grudgingly. Sometimes it happens that we ask someone for a favor as, for example, assistance with a task or to borrow something. The person ultimately does the favor, but with such a long face or with such obvious resentment, that we regret we ever asked. And usually such people never let us forget they did us a favor! No wonder St. Teresa of Avila often used to say, "From long-faced saints, deliver us, O Lord!"

On the other hand, if we ask someone else for a favor, and he or she gives it willingly, even cheerfully, we are greatly appreciative. Now, if we humans appreciate a spirit of cheerful giving, St. Paul assures us that God does too. Such cheerfulness in giving is a sign of the joy of the Holy Spirit.

JOY PROTECTS US FROM SPIRITUAL SADNESS AND TEMPTATION

The joy that comes from the Holy Spirit is a strong antidote to many spiritual ills and anxieties. It is indispensable for life-long growth in the spiritual life. We need to ask the Holy Spirit for this spiritual fruit to sustain us in the struggles and sacrifices of each day. Otherwise, these will discourage us and weigh us down.

St. Francis and the Importance of Spiritual Joy

St. Francis understood this very clearly. He developed in his life and in his teachings a comprehensive understanding of the importance of the joy of the Holy Spirit in our spiritual lives.

Spiritual Joy Should Characterize Every Christian

St. Francis, like St. Paul, took it for granted that joyfulness should be the ordinary state of mind and heart for every Christian. In his Rule of 1221, he described how his friars should conduct themselves:

> And all the friars, no matter where they are or in whatever situation they find themselves should, like spiritually minded men, diligently show reverence and honor to one another without murmuring. They should let it be seen that they are happy in God, cheerful and courteous, as is expected of them, and be careful not to appear gloomy or depressed like hypocrites. ("The Rule of 1221," ch. 8, *St. Francis of Assisi: Omnibus of Sources of the Life of St. Francis*, Quincy, IL: Franciscan Press, 1991, p. 38)

St. Francis loved spiritual joy, both in himself and in others. It was something he always strove to practice and wanted others, especially his friars, to do the same.

> It was always the supreme and particular desire of blessed Francis to possess an abiding joy of spirit outside times of prayer and Divine Office. This was the virtue he especially loved to see in his brethren and he often reproached them when they showed signs of gloom and despondency. (*Mirror of Perfection*, #95 in *ibid.*, p. 1229)

St. Francis Corrected Those Who Lacked Spiritual Joy

If he saw a friar who lacked spiritual joy and was filled with sadness, St. Francis corrected him:

> So the Father (St. Francis) used to censure those who went about with gloomy faces, and once rebuked a friar who appeared with a gloomy face, saying, "Why are you making an outward display of grief and sorrow for your sin? This sorrow is between God and yourself alone. So pray Him in His mercy to pardon you and restore to your soul the joy of His salvation, of which the guilt of your sins has deprived it. Always do your best to be cheerful when you are with me and the other brethren; it is not right for a servant of God to show a sad and gloomy face to his brother or anyone else." (*Mirror of Perfection*, #96, in *ibid.* p. 1230)

Spiritual Joy: A Strong Defense Against the Devil and His Temptations

Above all other reasons, St. Francis prized spiritual joy because it was a strong defense against the Devil and his cunning temptations. Gloominess emanated from the Devil, and whenever it inflicted spiritual sadness upon someone, spiritual joy won the victory. He used to remind his followers:

> The Devil rejoices most when he can snatch away spiritual joy from a servant of God. He carries dust so that he can throw it into even the tiniest chinks of conscience and soil the candor of mind and purity of life. But when spiritual joy fills hearts, the serpent throws off his deadly poison in vain. The devils cannot harm the servant of Christ when they see he is filled with holy joy. When, however, the soul is wretched, desolate, and filled with sorrow, it is easily overwhelmed by its sorrows or else it turns to vain enjoy-

ments. (*The Second Life of St. Francis* by Thomas of Celano, ch. 88, #125, in *ibid.*, p. 465)

Spiritual Joy: Results From Prayer And Purity Of Heart

For St. Francis, spiritual joy was the result of constant prayer and purity of heart. He urged his followers to be faithful to these two practices of piety so as to sustain their spiritual joy.

> If the servant of God strives to obtain and preserve both outwardly and inwardly the joyful spirit which springs from purity of heart and is acquired through devout prayer, the devils have no power to hurt him and they say, "We can find no way to get at him or hurt him, because this servant of God preserves his joy both in trouble and in prosperity." But the devils are delighted when they discover means to quench or disturb the devotion and joy which springs from true prayer and other holy practices.

> Therefore, my brothers, since spiritual joy springs from cleanness of heart and the purity of constant prayer, it must be your first concern to acquire and preserve these two virtues, so as to possess this inward joy that I so greatly desire and love to see both in you and myself, and which edify our neighbor and reproach our enemy. For it is the lot of the Devil and his minions to be sorrowful but ours always to be happy and rejoice in the Lord. (*Mirror of Perfection*, #95 in *ibid.*, p. 1229)

If he found himself in danger of losing his spiritual joy for any reason whatsoever, he immediately had recourse to prayer to sustain it. Here is how one of his biographers, Thomas of Celano, described his use of prayer to dispel sadness and restore joy:

> The saint made it a point to keep himself in joy of heart and to preserve the unction of the Spirit and the oil of gladness.

He avoided with the greatest care the miserable illness of dejection, so that if he felt it creeping over his mind even a little, he would have recourse very quickly to prayer. For he would say: "If the servant of God, as may happen, is disturbed in any way, he should rise immediately to pray and he should remain in the presence of the Heavenly Father until He restores unto him the joy of salvation. For if he remains stupefied in sadness, the Babylonian stuff will increase so that, unless it be at length driven out by tears, it will generate an abiding rust in the heart." (*The Second Life of St. Francis* by Thomas of Celano, #125, in *ibid*, pp. 465-466)

Spiritual Joy is Contagious

For St. Francis, spiritual joy and sadness had one quality in common: they were contagious. Their influence could easily spread to others. Whereas sadness might pull others down, joy could dispel sadness and lift people up. This is one of the reasons he was so insistent that the friars overcome any despondency or gloom. Their joy would be a source of inner strength to others.

Blessed Francis used to say:". . . Whenever I am tempted or depressed, if I see my companions joyful, I immediately turn away from my temptation and oppression and regain my own inward and outward joy." (*Mirror of Perfection*, #96 in *ibid*., p. 1230)

Spiritual Joy: Differs Greatly from Worldly Laughter

Finally, St. Francis taught in what spiritual joy consisted. He made a distinction between empty hilarity or excessive and worldly laughter, and truly profound spiritual joy.

It should not be imagined that our Father (St. Francis), who loved dignified and sensible behavior, wished this spiritual joy to be shown in levity or empty chatter, for these things are not evidence of spiritual joy, but of emptiness and folly. . . In one of his Counsels he gave an even clearer definition of the nature of spiritual joy in a servant of God saying: "Blessed is the Religious who has no pleasure or joy except in the most holy sayings and works of the Lord, and by these inspires men to the love of God in joy and gladness. And woe to the Religious who takes delight in idle and foolish talk, and by them provokes men to excessive laughter."

By a joyful face, therefore, he understood fervor, thoughtfulness, and the disposition and preparation of mind and body to a ready undertaking of every good work; for this fervor and readiness often have greater influence on people than the good deed itself. Indeed, however good an action may be, if it does not seem to have been done willingly and fervently, it tends to produce distaste rather than edification. So he did not wish to see a gloomy face, which often betrays a sluggish body and a melancholy mind. He always loved to see gravity of face and deportment both in himself and others, and did his best to encourage this by word and example. (*Mirror of Perfection*, #96, in *ibid.*, pp. 1230-1231)

Joy Gives Us an Attraction for the Spiritual Life

We also need spiritual joy to help us acquire an attraction for the spiritual life. Experiences at prayer, struggles to overcome our vices and root out our selfishness, and efforts to acquire virtues might easily seem too difficult and painful. They can readily become "repugnant." After all, we are more naturally attracted to material things than we are to those far greater but less obvious spiritual gifts that are known only through faith. So the Holy Spirit must assist us to acquire an inclination toward spiritual things. He must provide a joy or "spiritual sweetness" that will attract us away from the things of the flesh and move us toward the things of the spirit. Because we were made by God for Himself, He attracts us to Himself by His beauty and goodness.

Fervor Assists Prayer

We recognize a need for joy in prayer called "fervor" or "consolation." In the Scriptures we are told that we must taste and see that the Lord is good (Psalm 34:9). This fervor or sweetness makes prayer a delight. It is not boring, as many who have never seriously prayed tend to assume. It gives us a spiritual joyfulness which we cannot obtain from any other source. A classic example of this fervor was the experience of the two disciples who walked along the road to Emmaus with Our Lord on that first Easter. After they had recognized Him in the Eucharistic "breaking of the bread," they shared with each other the experience of fervor they enjoyed:

> Were not our hearts burning inside us as He talked to us on
> the road and explained the Scriptures to us? (Luke 24:32)

To talk with Jesus is what prayer is all about; to reflect on the Scriptures is a form of meditation, an aspect of prayer. As they did both these things with Jesus, the two disciples experienced such intense joy that their hearts were burning within them! Prayer was certainly not a difficulty that day!

As mentioned, the Holy Spirit gives us fervor or consolation to make prayer and other spiritual exercises attractive to us. When I was a novice, my novice director compared fervor to a piece of candy that parents may hold out to a little child to encourage the child to take his or her first steps. The candy is not the important thing; learning to walk is. But the candy can induce the child to take first steps, even very wobbly steps and even steps risking a fall, because the child wants the piece of candy. This is why beginners in the spiritual life often enjoy a period of "first fervor," a time when joyful consolation frequently accompanies their prayers and good actions.

Of course, as the child learns to walk, he will walk because he has to, and not for the candy. In a similar way, once we have learned to pray and are somewhat convinced of the necessity of praying in order to lead a faithful Christian life, God begins to withdraw His sensible consolation or fervor. The Holy Spirit will gradually wean them.

In the first place, the Holy Spirit does this so that we may begin to learn to pray out of conviction and not simply for the joyful feelings. As St. John of the Cross reminds us: "We must seek the God of consolations and not simply the consolations of God!"

Second, the Holy Spirit weans us off reliance on feelings of fervor so that our faith may grow. Faith is to believe even when we do not see. In regard to prayer, we might say that faith is to pray even when we do not have any feelings. We learn, in other words, to rely on trust in God's goodness, love, and fidelity. We gradually no longer depend on feelings, but on faith and trust in God.

This weaning off feelings is generally not a very easy process; in fact, it often proves to be a spiritual crisis for a lot of people. Many stop praying when they do not receive these joyful feelings. Sometimes this is because they are discouraged since there are no feelings to assure them that they are praying effectively. At other times, however, it is due to anger at God for withdrawing the consolations they have come to expect. To pray during times of spiritual dryness or "aridity" (absence of any joyful feelings) is a real trial. But this is when praying by faith instead of by feelings begins to grow stronger.

Furthermore, as we grow in faith, our prayer becomes more mature. The Holy Spirit with His seven-fold gifts begins to have a more obvious role in our Christian lives. This generally occurs after a period called "the dark night of the senses," during which time a person experiences longer bouts of dryness or aridity in prayer. Many do not persevere through these periods and give up praying.

If they do persevere, however, they will come to a more mature experience of prayer. The consolations in prayer will also be greater in proportion.

St. Teresa of Avila, one of the Church's greatest writers on prayer, distinguishes between the types of joy experienced in the initial stages of prayer and the joys of the more mature stages. The former she calls "consolations"; the Spanish word is "contentos." These are more emotional in nature and include feelings such as joy or peace or satisfaction. Though these feelings result from prayer or the practice of virtue, they are identical to similar feelings that we can experience in daily life situations. The latter joys she calls "spiritual delights"; the Spanish word is "gustos." These joys are more spiritual or mystical in nature and can only result from prayer. They have no natural counterparts.

To understand this difference more clearly, we can use a comparison from television. A child will probably find a good deal of pleasure in watching cartoons; the child's enjoyment will be very much on an emotional and sensory level. An adult, in contrast, might find great enjoyment in watching a suspense-filled drama (which would generally be unappealing to a child). The adult's pleasure is more intellectual and aesthetical than that of a child. The difference between the joy coming in prayer from emotional "consolations" and from "spiritual delights" is similar.

Joy Helps Us to Overcome Vices and Practice Virtues

What we have said about the joys at prayer applies also to the practice of virtues and the conquering of vices. The Holy Spirit's consolation gives us the strength and encouragement to keep up our daily struggles to do good and avoid evil. A good commander knows the need to rest his soldiers after battle; a good coach does the same for his players who have endured the heat of competition. In the same way, the Spirit of Joy refreshes us after our struggles and fortifies us to go forth again and give our best efforts.

THE "OIL OF GLADNESS"

Finally, I should mention here an ancient title given to the Holy Spirit: the "Oil of Gladness." Taken from the Scriptures (Psalm 45:8; Hebrews 1:9), it is applied to the Holy Spirit in a special way because He is compared to a fragrant oil that anoints us. The hymn, "Veni, Creator Spiritus" ("Come, Creator Spirit"), refers to the Holy Spirit as a "spiritual Anointing." The Golden Sequence, "Veni, Sancte Spiritus" ("Come, Holy Spirit"), refers to the Holy Spirit as "sweet Anointing here below."

This special title of the Holy Spirit as the Oil of Gladness is clearly described in an ancient Church document entitled the *Jerusalem Catecheses*. It was used to explain the meaning of the Sacrament of Baptism for those who were preparing to receive it. It first states that our own baptism makes us anointed ones, because it makes us like Jesus (and actually unites us to Jesus) Who is the Anointed One:[1]

> When we were baptized into Christ and clothed ourselves in Him, we were transformed into the likeness of the Son of God. Having destined us to be His adopted sons, God gave us a likeness to Christ in His glory, and living as we do in communion with Christ, Gods Anointed, we ourselves are rightly called the anointed ones. When he said: "Do not touch My anointed ones," God was speaking of us. (Cat. 21, *Mystagogia* 3, 1-3; p. 33, 1087-1091 as quoted in *The Liturgy of the Hours*, Vol. II, Catholic Book Publishing Co., New York, 1976 on pages 608-609)

The *Jerusalem Catecheses* then shows how both Jesus at His

---

[1] "The Anointed One" was the title the ancient Jewish people used to refer to the great leader God had promised to send to His People. The titles "Messiah" (from a Hebrew word) and "Christ" (from a Greek word), which refer to Jesus, both mean "the Anointed One."

baptism in the Jordan River and we in our Sacrament of Baptism are anointed by the Holy Spirit:

> We became the "anointed ones" when we received the sign of the Holy Spirit. . . Christ bathed in the river Jordan, imparting to its waters the fragrance of His divinity, and when He came up from them the Holy Spirit descended upon Him. . . So we also, after coming up from the sacred waters of baptism, were anointed with chrism[2], which signifies the Holy Spirit, by Whom Christ was anointed and of Whom blessed Isaiah prophesied in the name of the Lord: "The Spirit of the Lord is up on Me, because He has anointed Me. He has sent Me to preach good news to the poor" (Isaiah 61:1). (*Op. cit.*, p. 609)

Lastly, the *Jerusalem Catecheses* beautifully describes the Holy Spirit as the Oil of Gladness:

> Christ's anointing was not by human hands, nor was it with ordinary oil. On the contrary, having destined Him to be the Savior of the whole world, the Father Himself anointed Him with the Holy Spirit. The words of Peter bear witness to this: "Jesus of Nazareth, Whom God anointed with the Holy Spirit" (Acts 10:38). And David the prophet proclaimed: "Your throne, O God, shall endure forever; Your royal scepter is a scepter of justice. You have loved righteousness and hated iniquity; therefore God, Your God, has anointed You with the 'Oil of Gladness' above all Your fellows" (Psalm 44:7-8).

---

[2] "Chrism" is an oil solemnly blessed by the bishop of each diocese at a Mass called the Chrism Mass. This Mass was traditionally always offered on Holy Thursday morning, though now it can be anticipated earlier in Holy Week. This oil is the most sacred oil of the Church. It is used in the Sacraments of Baptism, Confirmation and Holy Orders, as well as in the consecration of sacred places (e.g., consecrated churches and altars) as well as sacred objects (e.g., consecrated chalices). Chrism consists of olive oil, balsam and other natural fragrances.

The oil of gladness with which Christ was anointed was a spiritual oil; it was in fact the Holy Spirit Himself, Who is called the Oil of Gladness because He is the source of spiritual joy. But we too have been anointed with oil, and by this anointing we have entered into fellowship with Christ and have received a share in His life. Beware of thinking that this holy oil is simply ordinary oil and nothing else. After the invocation of the Spirit, it is no longer ordinary oil but the gift of Christ, and by the presence of His divinity, it becomes the instrument through which we receive the Holy Spirit. While symbolically, on our foreheads and senses, our bodies are anointed with this oil that we see, our souls are sanctified by the holy and life-giving Spirit. (*Loc. cit.*, p. 609-610)

We can extend this idea of anointing with the Oil of Gladness, the Holy Spirit, to two other Sacraments: Confirmation confers the strengthening and enlightening presence of the Holy Spirit, while the Anointing of the Sick confers His healing presence. Both Sacraments are real sources of spiritual joy for those who receive them. Let us look at both sacraments briefly.

The conferring of the Holy Spirit in the Sacrament of Confirmation is by an anointing with the sacred oil called "chrism." After moistening his right thumb in the chrism, a bishop traces the Sign of the Cross on the forehead of the person to be confirmed, saying: "(*Name*), receive the seal of the Holy Spirit, the Gift of the Father."

In the Sacrament of the Anointing of the Sick, a priest anoints the forehead of a sick person with blessed oil called the "Oil of the Infirm." As he does this, he prays: "Through this holy anointing, may the Lord in His love and mercy help you with the grace of the Holy Spirit."

Finally, there is a spiritual or mystical sense in which we can speak of being anointed by the "Oil of Gladness." When we are inspired or prompted by the Holy Spirit, we may be said to be "anointed" with His spiritual oil. It is in these moments that we often experience the joy or gladness of the Holy Spirit's presence and working in us. We can truly say that the Spirit of Joy is the "Oil of Gladness" Who comforts and renews us in the service of the Lord and His people!

CHAPTER III

Openness to the Spirit of Joy

THE HOLY SPIRIT LOOKS FOR individuals who will be open to his presence and His working in them. He seeks those who listen with great faithfulness to His inspirations, and many times uses them for the furtherance of the divine plan of salvation.

SIMEON: OPEN TO THE SPIRIT

In the opening pages of St. Luke's Gospel, we meet one such person, a very holy man named Simeon. It was his privilege to publicly acknowledge Our Lord as a Light to the Gentiles and as the Glory of God's people, Israel (Luke 2:32). Despite his significant mission, we know very little about Simeon. But one of the things that immediately strikes us is his deep "life in the Spirit." St. Luke gives us this brief description of him:

> He was just and pious, and awaited the consolation of Israel, and the Holy Spirit was upon him. It was revealed to him by the Holy Spirit that he would not experience death until he had seen the Anointed of the Lord. He came to the Temple now, inspired by the Spirit, and when the parents brought in the Child Jesus to perform for Him the customary ritual of the law, he took Him in his arms and blessed God (Luke 2:25-28).

Let us look more closely at this brief description. The concept of being "just" meant to be a faithful observer of God's Law and thus someone who enjoys an intimate friendship with God. In biblical terms, it indicated a person of great holiness.[1] "Pious" meant to be prayerful, to possess a true spirit of worship and reverence toward God. We can well imagine that the possession of these virtues indicated a long life of faithful service to the Lord. The Spirit had been actively present within Simeon. On his part, Simeon had grown in openness and sensitivity to the inspirations of the Holy Spirit.

THE HOLY SPIRIT AT WORK IN SIMEON'S LIFE

Indeed, St. Luke identifies three important actions of the Holy Spirit in Simeon's life.

First, the Spirit inspired him to "await the consolation of Israel." The Spirit had stirred up an ardent longing for the promises of God. To "wait upon the Lord" for His promises is often very difficult because it is usually not a matter of waiting for a few days or weeks, but for months or years and perhaps even a lifetime. (Look at how long Abraham and Sarah awaited the fulfillment of God's promise that they would have a son through whom all their hopes would be fulfilled!) Throughout his long waiting, the Holy Spirit sustained Simeon by the joy of His consolation!

Second, Simeon's longing to see the promises of God fulfilled through the coming of the Messiah was rewarded. The Holy Spirit "revealed" to him that he would not die before seeing the "Anointed of the Lord." How was this revelation given? Possibly it was by some kind of an interior experience, perhaps by what we call an "inner locution." This occurs when a person hears God speaking in his or her heart. People who have genuinely experienced it know that this inner voice did not come from themselves. Or maybe Simeon

---

[1] St. Joseph himself is described briefly as "a just man" (Matthew 1:19).

simply experienced a growing inner conviction, a sort of "premo-nition" by which the Holy Spirit makes a person gradually aware of things to come.[2]

Third, in his openness to the Spirit's working in his daily life, Simeon was directed by the Holy Spirit to go to the Temple in Jerusalem on the very day Mary and Joseph were there to present the Christ Child.[3] There they all met!

This meeting between Simeon and the Holy Family was no coincidence. It was one of those "God-incidents" in life by which the Holy Spirit leads people into situations and circumstances that are grace-filled. Such people realize that they did not — and in most cases they could not, no matter how much they tried — ever bring about such spiritually enriching circumstances in their own lives. These mysterious workings are the result of God's loving Provi-dence. According to an old saying, "God orders all things sweetly."

SIMEON FORETOLD THE SORROWS OF JESUS AND MARY

What an overwhelming moment of joy it must have been when Simeon, a venerable old man, looked at the Christ Child, His Blessed Mother, and St. Joseph. St. Luke recorded the joy and peace in Simeon's heart in the words of his spontaneous canticle of praise and thanksgiving:

Now, Master, You can dismiss Your servant in peace; You have fulfilled Your word. For my eyes have witnessed Your

---

[2] St. Paul seems to have experienced this regarding the sufferings that awaited him. He testified to this when he said:

The Holy Spirit has been warning me from city to city that chains and hardships await me (Acts 20:23).

[3] According to ancient Jewish law, every first-born son had to be consecrated to the Lord. This was to commemorate the fact that the first-born male children of the Hebrews were spared when the "Angel of Death," passing over the land of Egypt at the time of the Exodus, struck down all the first-born male children of the Egyptians.

saving deed, displayed for all the peoples to see, a revealing
Light to the Gentiles, the Glory of Your people Israel
(Luke 2:29-32).

His life's longing had been accomplished; he was now at peace
to surrender his soul to the Lord. Yet, ironically, it is precisely at this
moment of his ecstatic joy that Simeon introduced the great
paradox of Christian life — namely, that all joy here on earth is
mingled with some sorrow. And so Simeon, filled with the Holy
Spirit Who had led him to the Temple, was now inspired to
prophesy the sorrows awaiting the Christ Child and His Mother:

> The Child's father and mother were marveling at what was
> being said about Him. Simeon blessed them and said to
> Mary His mother: "This Child is destined to be the down-
> fall and the rise of many in Israel, a sign that will be opposed
> — and you yourself shall be pierced with a sword — so that
> the thoughts of many hearts may be laid bare" (Luke 2:33-
> 35).

In this passage, Simeon says of Our Lord that He is destined
to be a "a sign that will be opposed," or in more familiar terms, "a
sign of contradiction." Jesus had come to give eternal life to all
people. He would give His life on the Cross for the salvation of the
whole world. Anyone could possess this new life simply by accepting Him and all He did and taught. Such persons would "rise" to
salvation and eternal life. But the contradiction is this: precisely
because some would close their hearts to Him and reject Him, they
would "fall" away from that gift of life in Christ and into eternal
death instead.[4]

---

[4] This contradiction is strikingly brought out in the Byzantine (or Eastern) crucifix. The
top part of the crucifix is basically like our Western crucifix, with the main crossbeam
supporting Jesus' arms and a small piece of wood at the top with the inscription, "Jesus
of Nazareth, King of the Jews." However, toward the bottom of the cross is a third
piece of wood. Nailed in the center it slants upwards on Jesus' right side and downward
on Jesus' left. As a reminder of Simeon's prophecy, the upward direction symbolizes

As recorded in St. Luke, Simeon next foretold Our Lady's own coming sorrows:

> And you yourself shall be pierced with a sword (Luke 2:35).

Our Lady, having so prayerfully pondered the inspired Word of God in Scripture, knew that the promised Messiah would have to suffer. How often she must have read the prophecies in Isaiah about the "Suffering Servant" Who was now her own Son:

> He was spurned and avoided by men, a man of suffering, accustomed to infirmity. . . It was our infirmities that He bore, our sufferings that He endured. . . He was pierced for our offenses, crushed for our sins. Upon Him was the chastisement that makes us whole, by His stripes we were healed. We had all gone astray like sheep, each following his own way; but the Lord laid upon Him the guilt of us all . . . Like a lamb led to the slaughter. . . He was silent and opened not His mouth (Isaiah 53:3-7).

Mary accepted the prophetic words of Simeon. In doing so, she also accepted that her life, intertwined as it was destined to be with that of her Son, would have its share of both joys and sorrows. Accordingly, traditional Catholic devotion to Our Lady acknowledges her having not only seven joys, but seven sorrows as well.

THE INESCAPABLE MINGLING OF JOY AND SORROW IN CHRISTIAN LIFE

Unnoticed, Simeon slips from the pages of Sacred Scripture as unassumingly as he had come into them. But the paradox of Christian life as a mingling of joy and sorrow remains. That paradox

---

those who will "rise" to eternal life because they accept Jesus and His Cross in their lives; the downward direction symbolizes those who will "fall" to eternal death because they reject Jesus and the Cross.

was an important part of the lives of Jesus and Mary, as presumably it was also of Simeon's. It must also become a significant part of our own lives if we choose to be near to Jesus and His Mother, and if we want to lead a fruitful life in the Spirit as Simeon did.

Joys and sorrows in life are like opposite sides of the same coin: they cannot be separated. In fact, the very sorrows we experience can become our joys in life. The Sacred Scriptures frequently repeat this theme. For example, in one of the Psalms we read:

> They go forth weeping, carrying the seed to be sown; they shall come back rejoicing, carrying their sheaves (Psalm 126:6).

The hard work of the farmer in planting and caring for his crops represents the sorrows of his life; but the harvest makes the effort rewarding, thereby giving joy to the farmer's heart. If the farmer did not make the effort to plow his field and plant his crops, there would be no harvest. St. Paul reminded the Christians at Corinth:

> Let me say this much: He who sows sparingly will reap sparingly, and he who sows bountifully will reap bountifully! (2 Corinthians 9:6)

We might well add: "If he does not sow at all, he will not reap anything." Bishop Fulton J. Sheen summed up the relationship between effort and reward, between sorrow and joy, very cleverly when he said: "There are only two basic philosophies of life: the Christian and the secularist. The Christian philosophy of life is: first comes the fast, then comes the feast! The secularist philosophy of life is: first comes the feast, then comes the hangover!"

THE PARADOX OF SORROW BEING TURNED INTO JOY

Our Lord highlights this theme of the intimate connection of joy and sorrow in the Christian life in His Last Supper discourse. He warns the Apostles (and us, too) in sobering and frank words:

> I tell you truly: you will weep and mourn while the world rejoices; you will grieve for a time, but your grief will be turned into joy (John 16:20).

Let's face it, suffering is a fact of life. It would be a serious illusion to believe we could totally insulate our lives from all sorrow, hurt, disappointment, tragedy, and failure. Sometimes we try to "bargain" with God so that we can get away from all such difficulties. We are willing to attend Mass, say our prayers, and in general "be good" if only we can be sure that God will approve of us and will not allow anything bad to happen to us. But life does not seem to bear this out. Even those very close to God have had a share in Jesus' Cross and suffering. Indeed, the closer they come to Our Lord, the more the shadow of His Cross seems to fall into their lives. As the examples of Our Lady and the Apostles show us in the Scriptures, bad things do happen to good people.

The key phrase in John 16:20 is Our Lord's telling us: "Your grief will be turned into joy." He does not say that our sorrow will be removed and replaced with a joy that is completely unrelated to our sorrow. He says that our sorrow will be turned into joy. This is not a replacement, it is a transformation! The sorrows shared with Jesus mysteriously become the key unlocking the joys of knowing and loving Him more deeply.

THE EXAMPLE OF OUR LADY'S "SPIRITUAL MOTHERHOOD"

Our Lord continues to develop this important teaching with a powerful comparison:

When a woman is in labor she is sad that her time has come. When she has borne her child, she no longer remembers her pain for the joy that a man has been born into the world. In the same way, you are sad for a time but I shall see you again; then your hearts will rejoice with a joy no one can take from you (John 16:21-22).

Our Lord draws His example from human life. A woman cannot give birth without suffering some of the pangs of childbirth. While the labor lasts, the pain can be intense, even overwhelming. But the joy of holding her child erases the memory of her anguish.

Some Scripture scholars suggest that when Our Lord spoke these words at the Last Supper perhaps He had in mind the "spiritual motherhood" His own Mother would undergo in less than twenty-four hours. Let us recall that because Our Lady was conceived without Original Sin, she did not suffer its punishment in the pains of childbearing when she gave birth to Our Lord at Bethlehem.[5] This is why it is our Catholic belief that the birth of Jesus from Our Lady was "virginal," that is, without the pain of childbirth and without the loss of her physical integrity.[6]

Now on Calvary, Our Lady would become a Mother again through the Redemption:

Woman, there is your son! (John 19:26)

---

[5] In the book of Genesis we read that the pains of childbirth were intensified as a result of Original Sin:

> To the woman He (the Lord God) said: "I will intensify the pangs of your childbearing; in pain shall you bring forth children" (Genesis 3:16).

[6] The Church speaks of three aspects of the "virginity" of the Blessed Virgin Mary. First, there is Mary's "virginal conception," by which we mean she conceived Jesus in her womb by the overshadowing of the Holy Spirit and not as the result of marital relations with St. Joseph, her spouse. Second, there is Mary's "virginal birth," by which she gave birth to Jesus without the loss of her physical integrity. (This is the meaning used here in the text.) Third, there is the fact that Mary remained a "virgin" perpetually after the birth of Jesus, never engaging in marital relations. This threefold "virginity" of Our Lady is often expressed in the phrase, "Mary was virgin before, during, and after the birth of Jesus."

This time, Our Lady was not spared the sorrow of "childbirth." She had to surrender her only natural Son in crucifixion, in order that she might become a spiritual Mother, a refuge, an intercessor for all her other adopted sons and daughters whom sin held in bondage.

What a powerful contrast! At Bethlehem, Our Lady became a Mother by giving natural life and birth to Jesus. At Calvary she became a Mother once again by sharing in the new spiritual birth and life of Jesus' disciples. At Bethlehem, Our Lady became the Mother of Jesus, the Head of the Mystical Body. At Calvary, she became once again the Mother of Jesus by becoming the Mother of His disciples, the members of the Mystical Body. At Bethlehem, Our Lady gave birth in joy. At Calvary, she gave birth in sorrow.

In one of his most famous sermons, St. Bernard of Clairvaux, with the power and beauty that often characterized his words, offered a prayer to Our Lady. It captures the intensity of that moment below the Cross for the Mother of Sorrows:

> Were those words: "Woman, behold your Son," not more than a sword to you, truly piercing your heart, cutting through to the division between soul and spirit? What an exchange! John is given to you in place of Jesus, the servant in place of the Lord, the disciple in place of the Master; the son of Zebedee replaces the Son of God, a mere man replaces God Himself! How could these words not pierce your most loving heart, when the mere remembrance of them breaks ours, hearts of stone and iron though they are! (St. Bernard, *Sermon on the Sunday within the Octave of the Assumption*, 14-15; *Opera omnia Edit. Cisterc.* 5 (1968), pp. 273-274 in *The Liturgy of the Hours*, Vol. 4, p. 1402)

Her joy now is to be a Mother to all of us and to bring us safely to her Divine Son! And this joy knows no bounds! Do we not experience a similar type of joy when striving for a vocation or a career in life? For example, doctors or nurses, spending long years in study, can easily get discouraged. The demands of study and sacrifice are many. They may well be tempted to give up. But once they attain their goal, they rejoice in the skill they have acquired. Their new profession will allow them to reach out now and help many other people.

In my long years of preparation for the Priesthood, I nearly became discouraged by a priest newly ordained about two weeks. I remember asking him if he was happy now that he had reached the goal of the Priesthood. I anticipated an answer filled with joy and excitement. Instead his answer was distressing. He said that if he had known all the suffering and sacrifice that was required to become a priest, he would never have become one! At some time, a bitterness or resentment seemed to have entered his heart. Such an attitude could easily destroy his potential for great joy in God's service. When I myself was ordained about six years later, Bishop Sheen made a very different comment: "The emotional thrill of your first Mass will fade with time, but your joy of being a priest — that grows!" How right he was!

THE PARADOX OF SORROW AND JOY
IS FOUND ULTIMATELY IN THE CROSS

This paradox of joy and sorrow in Christian life is symbolized by the Cross. How can we say that the Cross is the source of joy and not simply of sorrow in our Christian life? The secret is that we must first grow spiritually. This growth will change our attitude, our outlook.

To mature in Christ is akin to climbing a mountain. At the base of the mountain our view or perspective is quite limited. We cannot see over the trees and other objects that block our vision because we are on the same level. But as we climb the mountain, we begin gradually to see a broader panorama. At first we can begin to see over the obstacles at ground level. Then, as we go higher, we can see more and more of the scene around us. Finally, reaching the top of the mountain, we arrive at an unobstructed vantage point. We have achieved a panoramic view of the countryside around us.

As we journey spiritually, a similar experience happens regarding the meaning of Jesus' message of the Cross. To get beyond the ground level with its major obstacles to our vision, we first have to achieve some initial spiritual progress. We do this by struggling patiently with all the difficulties, temptations, trials, and sacrifices in our daily Christian lives. This teaches us to believe that there is always a God-given purpose to our suffering. We also begin to realize that through the crosses that come to us in life, God blesses us in many ways. They begin to "bear fruit" in our lives, and this helps to develop in us a greater sense of trust in God Who is always there to assist us.

We can also achieve a greater freedom from needless anxiety. Along with this usually comes a greater peace in life. We come to know through experience that worrying accomplishes little else than to disturb ourselves and those around us. At the same time, we come to recognize that God provides for all things in due order. Without realizing it, we are slowly climbing the "spiritual mountain," leading ultimately to the wisdom and joy Christ has promised through His Cross and ours. We come to realize the conviction expressed by Cardinal Newman, the famous English convert of the 19th century, who wrote:

> I will trust Him. Whatever I am, I can never be thrown away. If I am in sickness, my sickness may serve Him; in perplexity, my perplexity may serve Him; if I am in sorrow, my sorrow may serve Him. He does nothing in vain. He knows what He is about. He may take away my friends, He may throw me among strangers, He may make me feel desolate, make my spirits sink, hide my future from me — still He knows what He is about!

It is the Holy Spirit's role in our lives to help us use this paradox of sorrow and joy, or more precisely of sorrow turning into joy, to our spiritual advantage. He focuses us upon Jesus and the Cross. He makes us aware that the sufferings we endure have meaning for our life when we bear them in union with Jesus. These sufferings are not fatalistic or negative in tone; rather, they are redemptive and filled with hope. They are opportunities to grow further away from the world and closer to God. God uses suffering to free us more effectively and completely from the narcissistic self-centeredness that prevails in modern society so that we can become all that He has called us to be.

Let us return for a moment to the example of Simeon with whom we began this chapter. He knew the joy of the Spirit leading him into the Temple on that day of Jesus' Presentation. His joy was complete in seeing Jesus, the long-awaited Savior.

Yet, he also carried a prophetic message of sorrow and suffering for the Child Jesus and His Mother. Somehow he must have already integrated the two, joy and sorrow, in his own life. It would have been too great a conflict in himself to foretell such human sorrow and suffering to others while experiencing such ecstatic joy in himself. He could only have done this if he had already personally come to believe — through the enlightenment of the Holy Spirit and through his own experience in life — that sorrow in God's plan ultimately leads to joy in this life and in the next.

Recall Simeon's prophecy that Jesus would be "a sign of contradiction" leading to the "downfall" and the "rise" of many. Certainly "the sign of contradiction" in Jesus' life was most especially linked to the Cross. The Cross, so dreaded and despised, would become a paradox containing death and life, sorrow and joy, despair and hope, disbelief and faith, hatred and love.

It has been said that suffering can make a person better or bitter. It can become a stepping stone or a stumbling block on life's journey. The Holy Spirit, through the wisdom and love He pours forth into our minds and hearts, must teach us this important difference.

CHAPTER IV

The Paradox of the Cross and The Three Stages of the Spiritual Life

T HERE IS AN INEVITABLE experience at the heart of living our daily lives: all joy here on earth is always mingled with some sorrow. As an old Italian saying goes: "There is no rose without a thorn!" If we apply this experience to the daily living of our Catholic Faith, it means that if we want to share in Jesus'joy and glory, we must also be willing to share in His sorrow and suffering. To paraphrase the words of the spiritual classic, *The Imitation of Christ*, whoever wishes to eat the bread of joy with Jesus must also be willing to drink the cup of suffering with Him.

Jesus clearly lays down in the Gospel the essential conditions for anyone to follow Him:

> Jesus said to all: "Whoever wishes to be My follower must deny his very self, take up his cross each day, and follow in My steps" (Luke 9:23).

It is clear from both His teaching and His life that the preeminent symbol of Jesus and His Church is the Cross. Today the Cross can truly be called a "paradox." A paradox is something that at first appears to be a contradiction, but on closer observation one realizes it is really not so. Paradoxically, the Cross is at one and the same time the source of profound suffering and the source of indescribable joy! The Cross, for instance, is certainly a sign of suffering in Jesus' life. He voluntarily embraced the Cross, an instrument of torture and degradation devised by the ancient Romans, and He died upon it. He in turn tells us that to be His true disciples we must bear our "cross," our burdens and sorrows in daily life, our "share of the hardship which the Gospel entails" (2 Timothy 1:8).

The Cross, on the other hand, has now become a symbol of life, hope, and joy. Jesus turned His death on the Cross into a sign of His victory over sin, and even over death itself. The suffering and death of the Cross led Him to the glory and new life of the Resurrection. The Cross has now become a source of hope for all those who put their trust in Jesus. Although it seems a contradiction to its obvious meaning of sorrow, the Cross is the source of the most unique Christian joy.

We have already seen how Jesus will turn our sorrow in life into joy. In this chapter, we will look at how our attitude toward the message of the Cross and suffering in our daily Christian lives gradually changes as we mature spiritually. Under the influence of the Holy Spirit, our response to suffering can actually go from simple patience as a basic minimum Christian virtue to the attitude of perfect joy, a special gift of the Spirit of Joy.

THE TRADITIONAL THREE STAGES
OF THE SPIRITUAL LIFE

The prime example of growth in appreciating the message of the Cross is the experience of the twelve Apostles as it is told to us in the New Testament. According to the prominent spiritual writer, Father Reginald Garrigou-Lagrange, O.P., in his classic work, *The Three Stages of the Interior Life*, even the Apostles, like ourselves, had to pass through three different stages of spiritual growth. In classical spiritual writing, these are known as the Purgative, the Illuminative, and the Unitive stages or ways. It will be helpful if we look briefly at the essential elements of each stage.

THE PURGATIVE STAGE

The Purgative stage is the stage of beginners in the spiritual life. It is characterized by a general purification of the soul. During this stage a person begins his initial conversion to Christ by working to remove sin, especially all mortal sin and as far as possible even deliberate venial sin, from his life. He must also try to break the hold that sinful attachments to the world (avarice), the flesh (sensuality), and the Devil (pride) have on his life. To use St. Paul's expression, he "puts off his former way of life and the old self which deteriorates through selfish illusion and sinful desires, and puts on the new self by acquiring a fresh, spiritual way of thinking" (Ephesians 4:22-24).

During the Purgative stage, a person begins to practice the necessary virtues of the Christian life. He also begins to establish a prayer life through which he comes to know God in a very personal way. As he progresses in developing his relationship with God through prayer and the practice of virtues, he undergoes certain trials which the Lord may send to purify and strengthen him. In addition, his own acts of self-discipline and self-denial bring him eventually to a certain inner peace that the early Fathers of the Church called by the Greek word "apatheia." It means literally a state or condition "without passion."

Now that the unruly passions and sinful tendencies within him have been subdued and brought under control, a certain state of inner harmony or peace is achieved in his life. This peace, as St. Augustine described it, is the tranquillity of order. Such a person has begun to become inwardly free enough to sincerely know, love, and serve the Lord and others for His sake. His spiritual life has grown significantly, and he is ready to move ahead into the second stage of conversion.

THE ILLUMINATIVE STAGE

The Illuminative stage is that of people who are now advanced. The word illuminative indicates the idea of enlightenment. An interior light of the Holy Spirit is granted to the individual at this stage of his spiritual life. It is characterized by an increase of inner awareness and an appreciation of spiritual things. This is a time when the gifts of the Holy Spirit begin to work more fully in a person's life. The Holy Spirit helps the person to recognize the truths of our Faith through His gifts of Knowledge and Understanding. He also helps him to put these truths into practice in his daily life through His gifts of Courage, Piety, and Fear of the Lord. He strengthens the convictions of those who are striving to grow in holiness.

The prayer life of the person at this stage begins to undergo an important development. A person generally begins to experience the "dark night of the senses." In fact, this dark night is usually the entrance into the Illuminative stage. It is primarily a purification of our spiritual senses or feelings. In it, God withholds His emotional consolations and feelings of fervor at times of prayer, so that the person is drawn off dependence on them. He leads the person instead to greater reliance on faith. This strengthens the individual's prayer life. He becomes more consistent because he no longer prays when he "feels" like it, but now prays more constantly because he believes in its importance, and is convinced he needs to pray. This is usually the beginning of what is called "mystical" or contemplative prayer. Here, the activity of the Holy Spirit in the soul becomes more pronounced. The Holy Spirit moves the individual to be more aware of God's presence and to communicate with Him on a more familiar and intense level of prayer.

The person undergoes further purification by the "dark night of the senses." This is usually experienced as a prolonged series of trials in addition to dryness in prayer, such as situations of anger, temptations (especially against faith and chastity), and annoyances of all kinds. The whole purpose of these providential trials is to detach a person even further from the world and its vain attractions. Humility, charity, and patience grow deeper and stronger. The persons feels an ardent longing for God and for His promises. At the same time, he experiences an increased heartfelt desire to do all that he can to assist a neighbor's material and especially spiritual needs. All of this leads the person to the final stage of spiritual maturity.

The Unitive Stage

The Unitive stage is the stage of those individuals who have reached a full maturity or perfection of the spiritual life. The very word "unitive" expresses a state of continuous union with God. This intense union is brought about because the individual, with the generous help of God's grace, has grown so strong and constant in virtue that he avoids not only all deliberate sins against God and neighbor but as far as possible even the smallest faults and imperfections. He is so strengthened by the gifts of the Holy Spirit, especially Wisdom, that he becomes extremely generous in loving and serving the Lord and others. The person in this stage is operating on the level of the heroic virtues of the saints. He is willing to make any and every sacrifice necessary to give honor and praise to God, to help his brothers and sisters come closer to Him, and to deepen his own personal union with the Lord.

Such individuals also pass through another prolonged period of severe trials called the "dark night of the spirit." This is the final spiritual purification. It is often experienced in the form of very grave trials regarding faith, even feeling completely abandoned by God, or through trials of misunderstanding, rejection, and persecution. Often at this stage individuals see much of the good they have worked to accomplish in life now threatened with loss or destruction. But just as the sufferings at this stage will be great, so, too, will the consolations and joys.

In the Unitive stage there are incredible blessings, especially through experiences of deep mystical prayer. This could at times include such extraordinary phenomena as visions, ecstasies, even the stigmata[1], although these phenomena are not at all necessary. It is also a time when certain individuals are given exceptional apostolic and charismatic gifts[2], such as the working of miracles, bilocation, fragrance, prophecy, and the ability to read hearts.[3]

---

[1] Vision - This is a seeing by some kind of supernatural perception of someone or something that is not visible to our natural sight. For example, a vision of the Blessed Mother or of the Cross.

Ecstasy - This is a state which results from an overpowering spiritual experience in which a person's whole mental attention is fixed on some religious object, while his or her external senses are suspended, so that the individual cannot hear, see, smell, taste or feel anything outside. In some cases of ecstasy, persons have experienced their bodies rising somewhat off the ground; this is called levitation. For example, St. Joseph of Cupertino, a Conventual-Franciscan priest, was famous for his levitations.

Stigmata - This is the impressing of the five great wounds of Jesus (from His hands, feet and side) onto the body of another person. For example, St. Francis of Assisi was the first person known to have received these five wounds.

[2] Charismatic Gifts - There are two kinds of gifts given by the Holy Spirit.

(1) The first are His Sanctifying Gifts, which are given to assist the individual to grow in personal holiness. They are given along with Sanctifying Grace. Their purpose is to make a person open to receive and docile to follow the inspirations of the Holy Spirit. They are listed in Isaiah 11:2-3: Wisdom, Knowledge, Understanding, Counsel, Fortitude, Piety, and Fear of the Lord.

(2) The second are His "Charismatic Gifts," which are given to individuals not for their own sakes, but to be used by them to help build up the Mystical Body of Christ. In other words, they are given to meet the various needs of the Church community. Their exact number is disputed, but they are referred to in the Acts of the Apostles and in the writings of St. Paul. Spiritual writers often distinguish five categories of charismatic gifts: (1) instruction, (2) administration, (3) miracles, (4) service, and (5) prayer.

[3] Miracle - This is some awesome effect, known by our senses, produced by the supernatural power of God, surpassing what any known natural powers could ever produce. They are usually performed to confirm a truth or to manifest the holiness of someone. For example, Jesus' miracle of changing water into wine at the wedding feast of Cana.

Bilocation - This is the presence of someone in more than one place at the same time, brought about by God's power. For example, Padre Pio was known to appear in various places in the world, while yet being seen still at his friary in Italy.

Fragrance - This is one of various sweet-smelling scents given off from the person of saintly people. It is often referred to as the odor of sanctity. These scents have been

Usually in this stage, God mysteriously communicates to the person His intention to "wed" (= unite) his or her soul to Himself forever (an experience usually called the "spiritual betrothal"), and somewhat later He actually weds (= unites) the soul by some mystical experience (usually called the "spiritual marriage"). No doubt, these experiences flood the soul with ecstatic joy! An individual in the Unitive stage is often characterized by an all-pervading inner peace and security, so that despite severe temptations and trials raging outside himself, he remains tranquil and undisturbed within.

THE APOSTLES' GROWTH THROUGH THE THREE STAGES

As set forth in *The Three Stages of the Interior Life*, the Apostles, like all the rest of us, had to grow through three stages of spiritual maturing in their own personal lives. They were most privileged, however, to have had Jesus Himself as their "Spiritual Director."

From Their Call to the Time of Jesus' Passion

According to Father Garrigou-Lagrange, the Purgative stage of the Apostles' growth in holiness extended from the moment Our Lord called them to follow Him right up to the time of His Passion. This was the period when the Apostles first came to know Our Lord. They were privileged to witness His miracles, which gave them an

---

compared to the smells of fragrant flowers, perfumes or even incense. For example, many people testified that they experienced fragrance coming from the person of Padre Pio.

Prophecy - This is the accurate prediction of future events that could not have been known by any natural means. Many saints possessed this gift.

Reading Hearts - This is the ability to see the state of soul of another person in regard to such matters as its sins, hidden thoughts and intentions, and the like. For example, Padre Pio had this gift when he heard confessions.

understanding of His marvelous power as well as of His compassion for those in need. They heard His preaching, which allowed them to build up faith in what He taught them. They also had many opportunities for personal discussions with Our Lord. (We can actually call these "prayer experiences" since the Apostles were engaging in heart-to-heart conversations with Him, which is precisely what prayer is all about.)

This experience of being with Jesus was their initiation into a deeper relationship with Him. It was the beginning of their "first conversion." Their understanding grew to the point where they recognized Our Lord as the Messiah, the One Who had been sent by God with a special mission. As we shall see, it was also a time when they struggled with their own sinfulness and self-centeredness. They needed to deal with their anger, their jealousy, their pettiness, as well as their lack of concern, sensitivity, and compassion for others. They needed to learn to control their passions and correct their faults by beginning to practice the virtues Jesus was teaching them by His own words and example.

FROM JESUS' PASSION TO THE EVE OF PENTECOST

The second stage of the spiritual life of the Apostles began with the Passion of Jesus and it extended right up to the vigil of Pentecost. This period was the equivalent of the Illuminative stage of their spiritual development. Because the Lord Whom they loved was being taken from them, the Passion of Jesus caused the Apostles to undergo a profound crisis.

As we have already seen, those in the Illuminative way often experience what is called the "dark night of the senses." God takes away all sensible consolation or fervent feelings. It almost seems as if God disappears. He seems no longer to be with us. In fact, He may even appear to be quite far away. In the Apostles' case, they saw Jesus being taken away from them by His Passion. At the same time, in this moment of Our Lord's greatest need, the Apostles — despite their protests that they would be loyal to Him and even St. Peter's protest that he would die for Him — failed Jesus miserably. St. Peter himself denied the Lord three times; the other Apostles (except for the beloved disciple, St. John) fled in panic.

But the sorrow they all experienced afterwards because they had "disappointed Our Lord" stirred in them a profound repentance. This actually led them to a deepening of their own relationship to Jesus. It amounted to a "second conversion." Furthermore, Our Lord's appearances to the Apostles after His Resurrection encouraged them in their faith in Him. He consoled them with the gifts of His Easter joy and peace and with an initial bestowing of the Holy Spirit upon them (John 20:19-23).

Despite all of this, however, their spiritual life was not yet complete. Why? For one thing, they still had to deal with their fears; for another, there were still many things they did not yet understand; and finally, Our Lord had to prepare them to become His witnesses to the very ends of the earth. All of these considerations indicated that they still needed to receive the full outpouring of the strength and enlightenment of the Holy Spirit.

From the Coming of the Spirit at Pentecost

The Unitive stage of the Apostles' spiritual life began with the glorious coming of the Holy Spirit on Pentecost. This was like a "third conversion." Their first conversion started when Jesus called them. For example, He told Peter, Andrew, James, and John to leave their fishing boats and follow Him; He told Matthew to leave his tax collector's booth and follow Him. Their second conversion occurred as a result of the profound sorrow they experienced upon Jesus' Passion and Death, especially after they had denied Him and fled from Him in their fear and panic. This sorrow was likewise strengthened by the apparitions of the risen Christ to them.

Their third conversion occurred at Pentecost when they were

totally purified by the abundant pouring forth of the Holy Spirit upon them. With this third conversion, they entered the Unitive stage of their spiritual growth; they came to the perfection of the Christian life. With the grace of the Holy Spirit they were made mature in their discipleship. They became ready and willing to endure every sacrifice required of them for the love of Christ and for their own salvation. They became equally willing to endure great sacrifices in their zeal to work for the salvation of others by spreading to the ends of the earth the Good News about Jesus and the salvation He won for all of us.

CHAPTER V

The Paradox of the Cross:
Five Steps from Patience to Perfect Joy

W E HAVE JUST TRACED THE Apostles' spiritual growth through the Purgative, Illuminative, and Unitive stages as they experienced them. Now let us go back and retrace their spiritual growth in terms of their changed attitude toward suffering and toward Jesus' message of the Cross. How did they react when various trials and difficulties came their way? At each of the three stages, what degree of virtue were they able to practice when they met situations that required trust or sacrifice?

We find that as the Apostles sought to follow Jesus and put His teaching into practice, they progressively developed through different levels of virtue. They moved from being a group of fearful and uncommitted followers to a corps of fearless and dedicated disciples. Amazingly, as they grew in greater spiritual maturity, the Cross was no longer something to fear, no longer something from which to run. In fact, it became something that they wished to embrace just as Christ their Lord, their Master, their God, had embraced it before them.

In this chapter, we will follow the growth and development of the Apostles' awareness of the Cross in five ascending levels of virtue. At each of these five levels of virtue the Apostles experienced and reacted with different attitudes toward suffering. The five levels of virtue relate significantly to the three stages of spiritual growth.[1] The first level of virtue corresponds to the Purgative stage of the Apostles' spiritual formation. The second and third levels make up their Illuminative stage. The fourth and fifth levels form their Unitive stage. These same five levels of virtue are the very ones we ourselves must go through if we also wish to comprehend the message of the Cross, to appreciate it as the source of that unique joy which Jesus holds out to those who share the Cross with Him.[2]

---

[1] The following chart illustrates the parallel developments as described in this chapter.

3 Traditional Stages of the Spiritual Life	Corresponding Conversion Experience of the Apostles	Apostles' Attitude Toward Suffering & the Cross	Quality Level of Virtue
Purgative Stage	First Conversion: From their call to Jesus' Passion	Patience	Economy
Illuminative Stage	Second Conversion: From Jesus' Passion to His Ascension From Jesus' Ascension to Pentecost	Resignation Abandonment	Regular Plus
Unitive Stage	Third Conversion: Coming of the Holy Spirit At the end of their Spiritual Journey	Joy in Suffering Perfect Joy	Super Ultra

[2] As an aid to understanding, I shall designate each of these five levels with the same five labels that a leading gasoline company uses to distinguish its five grades of gasoline according to the level of octane present in each grade. Interestingly, octane is the element in gasoline that gives the engine more power and prevents hesitation and knock. As a result, the higher the octane, the smoother and more efficient the ride. The gasoline company designates its five ascending grades of octane as: economy, regular, plus, super, and ultra.

I shall identify the five ascending levels of virtue in appreciating the Cross with the same labels. Similar to the levels of octane, these five ascending levels of virtue enable us to deal with the Cross more effectively in our lives. As the power of virtue increases, our spiritual growth accelerates, so to speak, so that the earlier hesitancy caused by the Cross decreases while the fruit of the Cross — its unique joy — increases. Our spiritual journey, as a result, gets smoother, more consistent, and more efficient, too! These quality levels of virtue are already indicated on the chart in Footnote #1 above.

STEP ONE: PATIENCE

The first attitude of a Christian toward suffering and the Cross is the attempt to practice "patience." This is the economy level of virtue because it costs the least effort. It is characteristic of beginners in the spiritual life or of those in the Purgative stage. Patience comes from the Latin verb "patire" which means to suffer, to endure, to bear with. We all experience situations or persons who "test our patience," that is, they annoy us, do things to hurt us, cause us inconvenience, necessitate us to make sacrifices of all kinds. We feel a sense of frustration, followed by impatience and finally anger toward them for what we consider their thoughtlessness, selfishness, or even spitefulness. Attempting to live a true Christian life, we must respond to our feelings. This is when the battle begins within us. We try to gain control of our anger and impatience. It usually proves to be quite a struggle, and we may in the beginning have at best only a limited success or almost none at all.

The patience of this first level of virtue must go beyond simply an attitude of "grin and bear it." A person with such an attitude may put up with the difficulty only on the surface, only outwardly. But there is no real attempt in one's thoughts and feelings, in one's mind and heart, to try to come to grips with the disturbing person or situation. It can be no more than a stoic attitude, like the famous line of a comedian on TV years ago — "Don't fight it; it's bigger than both of us!" Or, it may be no more than an attitude of good riddance — "Simply go away, and leave me alone!" To be an expression of the true virtue of patience, it must go deeper.

When we are beginners, we hardly ever practice "perfect" patience, but we should try to learn some degree of patience with life's difficulties. At this stage, we will do a lot of vacillating back and forth in our determination to bear stressful situations patiently. We will feel strong, even compulsive desires to get out of this unpleasant situation. And we will probably be asking God constantly in our prayers to rescue us from our plight. The key to our growth in this first level of virtue, however, is that, although we may often lose our patience in situations that "test" us, we can have some degree of openness to correction and change. Such a sincere desire to do better can then translate into earnest attempts to improve ourselves and grow in authentic virtue.

At this stage, Christ's teaching about the Cross seems so difficult, so unreasonable, if not absolutely impossible to accept. It also seems so unnecessary, something we would feel much better not having to deal with.

EXAMPLES OF THE APOSTLES' NEED FOR PATIENCE

But we can take heart. This first level of struggle with impatience and with accepting the message of the Cross was even part of the Apostles' own experience as beginners in their spiritual lives. Despite having Our Lord's good example, clear teachings, and personal direction, they still had to struggle with their own self-centeredness just as we do. Such egotism certainly makes the practice of patience more difficult. Let us look at some Gospel examples.

The Apostles James and John once wanted Our Lord to call down fire and brimstone from Heaven upon a group of Samaritans who would not receive Him into their town (Luke 9:51-56). Our Lord reprimanded them sharply for their lack of patience and understanding. This was probably why He Himself nicknamed James and John "Boanerges" or "sons of thunder" (Mark 3:17).

On another occasion ten of the Apostles became indignant at James and John when their mother approached Jesus and asked to have her two sons sit in the first places of honor in the Kingdom of Heaven (Matthew 20:20-28). Jesus had to calm their anger and indignation. He then took advantage of the occasion to teach them that greatness in His Kingdom means humble service of their brothers and sisters.

Another example of the Apostles' lack of patience was their

petty arguing about who among them was the most important. Jesus used this occasion to repeat His teaching on the necessity of serving all our brothers and sisters. He then brought a little child into their midst to instruct them that the only way we can accept the Kingdom is with child-like simplicity (Mark 9:33-37; Matthew 18:1-5).

In two other situations some of the Apostles showed annoyance toward people who called out to Jesus while in desperate need. They showed impatience when a Canaanite woman shouted out after Jesus, entreating His help. The disciples told Our Lord: "Get rid of her. She keeps shouting after us" (Matthew 15:21-28). The Apostles were likewise annoyed with the blind man named Bartimaeus. As Jesus was walking near him in a crowd, Bartimaeus called out to Jesus to pity him in his affliction. Instead of encouraging Bartimaeus, some of the Apostles at first "sternly ordered him to be quiet" (Luke 18:39). It was only after Our Lord Himself called Bartimaeus over that these same Apostles, along with some of the crowd, gave him any encouragement: "You have nothing to fear from Him. Get up. He is calling you" (Mark 10:49).[3]

These examples reveal that even the Apostles themselves, in their early years of discipleship, had much changing and maturing to do in their spiritual life. They needed a lot more patience. They required further ongoing conversion.

The Need to Conquer Self-Love

Their need for further conversion was due to two factors.

First, it was because they had not yet sufficiently conquered their self-centered love. They easily gave vent to their impatience when things did not go their way. To conquer such self-love, however, is precisely the main task of a person in the Purgative stage. Only when he has fought against his own selfishness and

---

[3] This attitude of the Apostles toward these persons in such need reminds me of an old saying: "I was down and you pushed me further!"

passions and brought them somewhat under control, can there be any degree of peace in his soul. This peace, called "apatheia," allows him to practice the different virtues more freely and more consistently. The Apostles were not yet at that point. They were still in the Purgative way, but they were making progress. They listened to Our Lord's corrections, and they responded with openness to what Our Lord was teaching them.

The Need for the Spirit to Work More Fully

The second reason why the Apostles still needed much more ongoing conversion was the fact that the work of the Holy Spirit in their lives was, as yet, minimal. The Holy Spirit, working through His seven-fold gifts and many inspirations, only gradually becomes more evident in a person's life. This occurs when a person's passions and selfish love, which block the Holy Spirit from working freely in one's life, are conquered. This initial stage of purification from one's egotism allows the Holy Spirit more room to operate effectively. The obstacle is not on the Holy Spirit's part; there is no inability or ineffectiveness of His power or gifts. Rather, the difficulty is on the part of the individual. As long as self-centered love and the dominance of one's own passions continue, a person is not free to respond wholeheartedly and consistently to the Spirit's inspirations. The conversion process must go on.

Through all of this, what was the Apostles' attitude toward Jesus' message of suffering and the Cross? At this point, they found it hard to accept the message of the Cross as Jesus preached it. The Gospels clearly show this. The Synoptic Gospels — Matthew, Mark and Luke —each record three separate predictions by Our Lord of His impending suffering, Death, and Resurrection. Despite its repetition, the Apostles did not grasp this message. St. Peter tried to talk Jesus out of the Cross the first time He mentioned it (Matthew 16:21-23). After the second prediction, the Apostles "were overwhelmed with grief" at Our Lord's words (Matthew 17:23). They could not understand the warning of Jesus and they were afraid to question Him on what He meant (Mark 9:32, Luke 9:45). In regard to Our Lord's third prediction of His impending suffering, which was soon to occur in Jerusalem, St. Matthew and St. Mark record no response at all on the Apostles' part, whereas St. Luke sums it up:

> They understood nothing of this. His utterance remained obscure to them, and they did not grasp His meaning (Luke 18:34).

Maybe they simply did not want to understand. When some truth or reality appears to be too painful to bear or to deal with, keeping it obscure makes it seem less threatening or at least safer to handle. But sooner or later the bubble will burst and reality will hit full force. It did for the Apostles with the actual death of Jesus. But, ironically, Jesus' Death actually became the opportunity for a tremendous step forward in their spiritual lives.

STEP TWO: RESIGNATION

The second attitude of a Christian toward suffering and the Cross is "resignation." This is the regular level of virtue because it should become the attitude of a mature Christian. It is characteristic of those who are somewhat advanced in the spiritual life, of those who are entering upon the Illuminative way. Resignation is the virtue of patience brought to a fuller and more developed state. Resignation implies a certain degree of firmness or consistency in the practice of patience. It includes also the willingness (more or less) to accept the present difficulty or trial. There may still be strong feelings against suffering and even a wish that it would be removed. But as long as it continues one sees it as willed or at least as permitted by God; he or she is therefore willing to accept the reality of it for as long as it must be endured. This virtue of resignation is reflected in the popular "Serenity Prayer":

Lord, give me the serenity to accept the things I cannot change, the courage to change the things I can, and the wisdom to know the difference.

We acquire resignation by trying patiently, for the love of God, to put up with whatever difficulties He allows to come our way in life. It usually emerges only after long struggles to curb our anger, annoyance, criticalness of others, and complaining. It requires us to let go of our own preferential ease and comfort. It becomes possible through a growing awareness that our crosses in life can actually contain some good through which we can grow spiritually.

EXAMPLES OF THE APOSTLES' RESIGNATION

The Apostles came to this level of virtue through the Passion, Death, and Resurrection of Our Lord. We must realize what an enormous effect these events had on them. Time and again Jesus had tried to warn the Apostles of his impending suffering and Death. As we saw, however, they could not grasp what He was saying. Furthermore, being afraid to ask Him for any clarification, they lulled themselves into a false sense of security. After all, was not Jesus with them? What did they have to fear?

Actually the storm clouds were gathering for some time. Finally, on Holy Thursday night, the storm broke full fury. The Lord was seized. The Apostles, realizing the grave danger of being His followers, fled for their lives in sheer panic. Most of all, St. Peter, who at the Last Supper had professed his readiness to face imprisonment and death for Jesus (Luke 22:34), three times denied he even knew Him.

They Experience a "Second Conversion"

But the sorrow and repentance of St. Peter began immediately after his denials. St. Luke tells us what happened when Peter had just denied Our Lord for the third time:

The Lord turned around and looked at Peter, and Peter remembered the word that the Lord had spoken to him, "Before the cock crows today, you will deny Me three times." He went out and wept bitterly (Luke 22:61-62).

Our Lord's look was not one of reproach and condemnation; not "Peter, how could you do such a thing?" Rather, it was a look of compassion and mercy, "Peter, I tried to warn you, but you would not listen. Peter, I forgive you." According to an ancient tradition, whenever St. Peter afterward heard a rooster crow, he shed many tears, remembering his denials of the Lord he loved so much. The sorrow that St. Peter felt was so profound that it actually served to cleanse his soul of any remaining self-love or self-complacency.

We can assume that a similar sorrow and repentance occurred in the hearts of the other Apostles who had fled in fear. Their sorrow served as a "dark night" experience, purifying their self-love, their pettiness, their ambition, their impatience with others' weaknesses and shortcomings, for they now had to look at their own. All of this served as a profound "second conversion" experience. The overwhelming sorrow of Jesus' Passion and Death purified them of their self-centered love. They were truly advancing in virtue. Their attitude toward suffering and the Cross was also changing. They were no longer fleeing from the Cross.

They are Strengthened by the Joyous Presence of the Risen Lord

For forty days after Easter, the Apostles enjoyed the privilege of seeing the Risen Lord on several occasions. His appearances on Easter Sunday alone were overwhelming in the joy, strength, and consolation they conveyed. There were the appearances early on Easter morning to St. Mary Magdalene and the other women at the tomb who reported the good news of Jesus' Resurrection to the Apostles. There was also the appearance to the two disciples on the road to Emmaus. At first the disciples did not recognize Jesus; but their hearts burned within them as He spoke to them and as He opened their minds to understand the Old Testament Scriptures that applied to Him. They also experienced Jesus as risen and recognized Him as He "broke the bread" with them, a reference to His celebrating the Eucharist with them. Finally, Jesus appeared to the Apostles on Easter night. What a joyous reunion: they were "incredulous for sheer joy and wonder" (Luke 24:41). He bestowed upon them His gift of Easter peace. He also breathed upon them and conferred the Gift of the Holy Spirit, along with the power to forgive sins. He had died to atone for all sins; now He gave His Apostles the power to forgive sins in His Name.

There were other appearances of our Risen Lord: to St. Thomas, to remove his doubts and change his skeptical attitude; to a group of the Apostles when they were fishing and could catch nothing without His help; to St. Peter in the emotional scene of Jesus asking him three times, "Do you love Me?" and three times Peter renewing his profession of love and loyalty to Jesus.

Their virtue had grown and would continue to do so. Still, their faith needed to be strengthened, their love to be made more secure. Further, there were many things they still could not grasp. Nonetheless, their spiritual lives were doing better. They had certainly grown. They had come to realize a great deal merely by reflecting on the facts of Jesus' Death and Resurrection. Having the awareness of His risen presence among them gave them hope.

Finally, there was one other very important change in them. They were no longer running away! Their virtue had reached the level of "resignation." Knowing that Jesus was still with them, they were resigned to whatever might come. The locked doors of the place where they were staying, however, showed that their fear of being persecuted as Jesus' followers was not yet completely removed. Whatever wisdom and courage they still needed would only be given with the fullness of the Holy Spirit's coming at Pentecost.

STEP THREE: ABANDONMENT

The third attitude of a Christian toward suffering and the Cross is "abandonment." This is the "plus" level of virtue because it implies that an extra effort has been made. It is characteristic of those who have already progressed well into the Illuminative stage. Abandonment is a complete entrusting of one's self to God, allowing Him to be totally in charge of one's life. By it a person places himself completely into God's hands!

This was certainly the attitude of Our Lady at the Annunciation when she acknowledged herself to be the handmaid of the Lord. By this she was telling the angel that her heart was so disposed to God, to His glory and His will, that she was ready to do whatever He would ask of her. This included on her part a readiness to sacrifice or suffer all that doing His will might entail. Our Lady, then, is a model of total abandonment. She perfectly imitates the attitude of her Divine Son of Whom we read that on coming into the world, He stated that He had come to do the Father's will (Hebrews 10:9).

A Deep Trust in Divine Providence

Abandonment involves a deep trust in Divine Providence and its mysterious working. It rests on the conviction expressed by St. Paul that if we truly love God, all things will work together for some good, for ourselves as well as for others (Romans 8:28).

God only permits evil to exist in order to bring some greater good from it. Did not God permit the Original Sin of our first parents, a sin which has affected every person in the human race except Our Lord and His Holy Mother, in order to send us His own Divine Son as our Redeemer? The graces flowing from Jesus' redemptive death have been far more abundant than if our first parents had never sinned and He had no need to die for the salvation of all. Using a quote from St. Augustine, the Church praises God in her joyous Easter Proclamation:

O happy fault, O necessary sin of Adam, which gained for
us so great a Redeemer!

God Only Sends Us What We Can Handle

A further point about Divine Providence is that God gives us
only what we can handle by way of trials and sufferings. He knows
how much each of us can bear. St. Paul clearly expresses this
conviction:

> God keeps His promise. He will not let you be tested
> beyond your strength. Along with the test He will give you
> a way out of it so that you may be able to endure it (1
> Corinthians 10:13).

We do not always know what each person can endure, but
God does. Sometimes we think someone might be very strong and
capable; yet, under trial, he may crumble easily. So God deals with
that person more gently. He lays a lighter burden on his shoulders.
On the other hand, some people appear quite frail and timid, and
yet under trial, they prove amazingly strong and faithful.

St. Francis de Sales, certainly no stranger to trials, summed up
this aspect of the Cross by saying it always comes "custom-fitted" to
each individual:

> The everlasting God has in His wisdom foresaw from
> eternity the cross that He now presents to you as a gift from
> His inmost Heart. This cross He now sends you He has
> considered with His all-knowing eyes, understood with
> His divine mind, tested with His wise justice, warmed with
> loving arms, and weighed with His own hands to see that
> it be not one inch too large and not one ounce too heavy
> for you. He has blessed it with His holy Name, anointed it
> with His grace, perfumed it with His consolation, taken
> one last glance at you and your courage, and then sent it to
> you from Heaven, a special greeting from God to you, an
> alms of the all-merciful love of God.

In regard to suffering, abandonment goes even further than resignation. In a sense, it builds upon it and perfects or completes it. Resignation deals with the past and the present; abandonment extends even into the future. In other words, one becomes resigned to bearing with difficulties and sufferings that have either already come his way or are still affecting him. One makes his peace by accepting whatever already was or still is. Abandonment, on the other hand, is the willingness to accept even beforehand whatever God may choose to send in the future. It demands a high level of trust. Mother Teresa of Calcutta expresses what has to be a perfect summary of abandonment[4] when she says: "We must take all that God gives, and give all that He takes, with a smile!"

Our Lord teaches us that fear is useless but that trust is absolutely necessary (Mark 5:36). Fear is characteristic of beginners in the Purgative stage. If trust does not gradually replace fear and grow stronger, a person will never reach this more mature attitude of the spiritual life. A person with such trust really accepts the fact that he is never alone in facing trials. A retreat director once told me, "No matter who or what you face in life, if God is with you, you are always in the majority." I have never forgotten his words of wisdom. Trust inspires the confidence that with God's help all obstacles, big or small, can be overcome. Like the popular little prayer says, "God, help me to remember that nothing is going to happen to me today that You and I together can't handle."

Job, Model for Abandonment

This disposition of "abandonment" is clearly seen in the figure of Job in the Old Testament. He was certainly tested by fire! Many reputable Scripture scholars believe that Job is more a literary figure

---

[4] Other expressions of abandonment by saintly persons would be:
    (1) St. Francis de Sales summed up his spirituality in his motto: "Seek nothing, refuse nothing."
    (2) The Servant of God, Father Solanus Casey, O.F.M. Cap., would frequently say: "Blessed be God in all His designs."

than an actual historical person as such. If he were a real person, the language and situations as presented have no doubt been greatly exaggerated to create a dramatic impact on the reader, and they certainly do.

The Book of Job was written to help the Jewish people come to a balanced religious attitude toward suffering. It was especially directed at the problem of suffering by innocent people. It attempts to answer the age old question, "Why do bad things happen to good people?"

Job is presented as an extremely devout and moral man, blessed with a large family and enjoying great material prosperity. For no apparent wrongdoing on his part, everything is taken away from him — all his possessions are destroyed or stolen, all his children are tragically killed. When told of all these misfortunes, one following upon another in dramatic succession, Job responds humbly in an attitude of total abandonment:

> Job cast himself prostrate upon the ground and said, "Naked I came forth from my mother's womb, and naked shall I go back again. The Lord gave and the Lord has taken away; blessed be the Name of the Lord." In all this Job did not sin, nor did he say anything disrespectful of God (Job 1:20-22).

Later on, when Job is afflicted with terribly painful boils from head to foot, his own wife accuses him of being guilty of some terrible sin. Otherwise, why is he being so severely punished? But Job humbly maintains his moral innocence. When his wife suggests that he should curse God for allowing all these afflictions and then die, Job again answers with an attitude of complete abandonment:

> "We accept good things from God, and should we not accept evil?" Through all this, Job said nothing sinful (Job 2:10).

We have already observed that abandonment is the perfection of resignation, including not only the past and present, but even the future. We see this in Job's whole attitude. His resignation is seen in his complete acceptance of all the evils God permitted to happen to him. His abandonment is expressed in his being ready to accept any good or evil that might come from God's hand. St. Francis de Sales once commented that it did not matter to Job whether it was good or evil that came to him; what did matter, however, was that it came to him from the hand of God. St. Francis de Sales labeled this the "permissive will" of God by which He may permit an evil such as war to happen, even though He does not really want it; God permits such a thing to happen in order to bring some greater good out of it.

A Word of Caution

Before passing on to the experience of the Apostles, there is another important comment we must make about Job. We have already mentioned that Job is essentially a literary figure. He is intended to present to the Jewish people the embodiment of the "ideal" attitude of trust and surrender to God in times of suffering. Now, Job appears to express no immediate sorrow upon hearing of the death of his children. This seemingly stoic passivity to human emotions would be frightening were we expected to act in this way.[5]

We all have to grow or work our way up to both resignation and abandonment, especially in the face of human suffering. Maybe it will take us a long time to accept a cross of misfortune, disappointment, separation, injury, death, or whatever. Through it all, however, there is no doubt that we will experience real pain and sorrow. After all, even Our Lord Himself wept at the death of His dear friend Lazarus (John 11:35-36), and He was certainly not less abandoned to His Heavenly Father's will than Job was! Even the

---

[5] In our own human experience, we all tend to suffer with far more emotion than Job. Such passivity reminds me of a sign that my youngest brother, Michael, had on his desk when he was a college student: "I promise. . . to be good. . . to be careful. . . not to lie. . . not to swear. . . not to drink. . . not to smoke. . . not to cheat. . . not to go out with the opposite sex. The funeral is tomorrow!"

saintly stigmatist, Padre Pio, no stranger to intense suffering, wept
for days over the death of a very close doctor-friend who had helped
him build a hospital for the poor near his friary. Another friend tried
to pull the Padre out of his sorrow by saying, "After all, Padre Pio,
don't you think the doctor is in Heaven?" The Padre answered,
"Certainly he is! But not only the mind demands its part, so does
the heart." In other words, we humans have more than an intellectual existence; we cannot live just from the neck up. We have our
emotions, and sorrow is one of them. They must have their own
legitimate expression. To experience the emotion of sorrow in the
midst of profound suffering is absolutely essential, because it is
absolutely human.

EXAMPLE OF ABANDONMENT ON THE PART OF THE APOSTLES

How did the Apostles practice abandonment? We have
already seen how they grew from patience to resignation through
the effect of the painful mystery of Jesus' Death and the overwhelming joy of His Resurrection. This resignation became abandonment
when Jesus told them at His Ascension that they would become His
witnesses, beginning in Jerusalem and Judea, then in nearby Samaria,
and finally to the ends of the earth (Acts 1:8). He commissioned
them with authority to preach to all men and women. They were
to make disciples of them, and they were to baptize all those who
believed in the Name of the Blessed Trinity. They were to carry out
everything He had taught them (Matthew 28:18-20).

By the very fact that they accepted this commission, the
Apostles put the whole future of their lives into Jesus' hands. They
knew this would not be easy. They understood clearly that there
would be many hardships in travel, privations of food and shelter,
discouraging results, much opposition and even violent persecution. After all, Jesus had told them when He sent them out on their
first missionary journey:

I am sending you out as lambs in the midst of wolves (Luke 10:3).

Having lived through the violence of Jesus' Passion and Death, they grasped even more clearly His warning to them at the Last Supper:

If you find that the world hates you, know it has hated Me before you. If you belonged to the world, it would love you as its own; the reason it hates you is that you do not belong to the world. But I chose you out of the world. Remember what I told you — no slave is greater than his master. They will harry you as they harried Me. They will respect your words as much as they respected Mine (John 15:18-20).

Despite all that they knew awaited them, the Apostles did not run away. They stood their ground. They were now ready to serve Jesus no matter what He would ask of them, no matter where He sent them, no matter what sacrifices they had to make for His sake and for the sake of His Kingdom. The Apostles placed their lives on the line because they knew they would not go forth alone; Jesus would be with them.

Know that I am with you always, until the end of the world (Matthew 28:20).

Obedient to Jesus' command to remain in Jerusalem until they had received the promise of the Father and power from on high, the Apostles prayed fervently for the Gift of the Holy Spirit. They joined in earnest, unceasing prayer with Our Lady, with some of Jesus' relatives, and with a group of men and women disciples (Acts 1:13-14). What longing there must have been for the Spirit to come! How eager they were to begin preaching the Good News about Jesus, especially about His saving Death and glorious Resurrection. They were ready to hold back nothing of themselves. This is total abandonment.

STEP FOUR: JOY IN SUFFERING

The fourth attitude of a Christian toward suffering and the Cross is joy in suffering. This is the super level of virtue because it adds a special element of joy over and above the readiness to accept what comes. It is characteristic of those who have reached the heights of the spiritual life in the beginning of the Unitive stage.

"Spiritual Joy" — What It Is Not

Such "spiritual joy" must be carefully understood, so as to avoid any false or distorted notions. It has nothing to do with any self-inflicted pain or punishment which some people may impose on themselves out of feelings of self-hate or self-rejection. Such people are mistakenly convinced that they "deserve to suffer," and so they find some kind of morbid delight in afflicting themselves for their past guilts of all kinds. They assume that God will feel "better" if they feel "worse." This is nowhere near the Christian notion of "joy in suffering."

Nor is it any form of "self-pity," feeling sorry for one's self either because things have never really turned out one's way in life, or because others always seem to have gotten the better deal. In such cases, a morbid delight may follow which has absolutely nothing in common with true spiritual joy.

Christian "joy in suffering" does not come from any masochistic attraction to pain; after all, suffering in itself has no value. Rather, this joy is rooted in the motive for enduring such suffering, namely, in an intense love for God, as well as for one's neighbors and their welfare.

Let us take the example of St. Maximillian Kolbe. It is said that he had a great fear of suffering. Yet, prompted by the grace of the Holy Spirit, he voluntarily offered his own life to save a fellow prisoner who was condemned to die in a Nazi concentration camp. For his volunteering, Fr. Kolbe spent ten days in a starvation bunker. He willingly and even joyfully suffered for the good of his neighbor, perfectly fulfilling Jesus' words:

> There is no greater love than this, to lay down one's life for one's friends (John 15:13).

Do not be mistaken; he suffered physical pain and a lot of it. Love did not take away the pain, but it gave a purpose for enduring it willingly. In this way his motivation of love became a source of surpassing joy on a spiritual level.

CHRISTIAN JOY SPRINGS ONLY FROM LOVE

This uniquely Christian form of joy springs entirely from the motive of love. No one can reach the heights of the Unitive stage unless his will, which makes the choice to love, has become deeply rooted in both the love of God and the love of one's neighbor. It is a love purified of all the alloys of selfishness. It is the love that brings us to that "purity of heart" by which we are led to see and evaluate all things from God's perspective alone. It is a love that sees all things in God and God in all things.

This love and this joy are the fruits of the Holy Spirit working in the depths of the soul. He produces these powerful effects in those who have become totally detached from the world's vain pleasures and possessions, as well as faithfully responsive to His inspirations. In this way the Holy Spirit will direct them to grow in an ever-increasing generous service of God and one's neighbor. Such dispositions are summed up in a popular prayer written by St. Ignatius of Loyola, often called "A Prayer For Generosity":

> Teach us, good Lord, to serve You as You deserve; to give and not to count the cost; to fight and not to heed the wounds; to toil and not to seek for rest, to labor and not to ask for any reward save that of knowing that we do Your will. Amen.

The Apostles experienced this growth in generous love on Pentecost. As we have seen, they had already experienced two "conversions." The first was when Jesus called them to follow Him; the second was brought on by both the profound sorrow at Jesus' Death and the unspeakable joy of His Resurrection. Now, on Pentecost they experienced their "third conversion," which was brought about by the abundant outpouring of the promised Gift of the Holy Spirit. He made it possible for the Apostles' love to reach a height of generosity which they could never have attained through their own efforts alone.

This outpouring of the Holy Spirit brought about a profound purification from fear and selfishness. This is seen on Pentecost when the Apostles — who little more than fifty days before had fled for their lives from the Garden of Olives rather than be seized as Jesus' disciples — publicly went out and before a vast crowd and fearlessly preached Jesus as Lord and Messiah:

> All were filled with the Holy Spirit. They began to express themselves in foreign tongues and make bold proclamation as the Spirit prompted them (Acts 2:4).

Some days after Pentecost we see even more evidence of how much the Apostles changed through the power of the Holy Spirit. St. Luke in Acts records the cure of a crippled man by St. Peter and St. John. Because of this cure and St. Peter's subsequent sermon stressing the Resurrection of Jesus, the Jewish leaders in the Sanhedrin angrily interrogated both Apostles. The two Apostles were undaunted. St. Peter confidently spoke in the power of the Holy Spirit with Whom he was filled (Acts 4:8). Even the Jewish leaders recognized the unlikely confidence of two fisherman to speak so assuredly in their presence:

> Observing the self-assurance of Peter and John, and real-
> izing that the speakers were uneducated men of no stand-

ing, the questioners were amazed. Then they recognized these men as having been with Jesus (Acts 4:13).

When the authorities resorted to threats of punishment to forbid the Apostles from ever again preaching to the people about Jesus, the Apostles were not in the least impressed:

> Peter and John answered: Judge for yourselves whether it is right in God's sight for us to obey you rather than God. Surely we cannot help speaking of what we have heard and seen (Acts 4:19).

St. Luke assures us that they continued to preach the Word of God with great confidence because they were filled with the Holy Spirit (Acts 4:31).

The final sign of the transformation of the Apostles came when all of them were put on trial before the Sanhedrin for defying the ban against preaching to the people about Jesus (Acts 5). After much discussion, the Sanhedrin reluctantly agreed not to kill the Apostles, but to let them go free. But before they were set free, the Sanhedrin decided to teach them a lesson and ordered the Apostles to be scourged.

> The Sanhedrin called in the Apostles and had them whipped. They ordered them not to speak again about the Name of Jesus, and afterward dismissed them. The Apostles for their part left the Sanhedrin full of joy that they had been judged worthy of ill-treatment for the sake of the Name (Acts 5:40-41).

Here we find the joy in suffering that characterizes the hearts of those deeply in love with God. What growth and change has taken place within the Apostles in such a short period of time through the Holy Spirit! St. Paul writes about the Spirit:

> The Spirit God has given us is no cowardly Spirit, but rather One that makes us strong, loving and wise. There-fore, never be ashamed of your testimony to Our Lord, nor

of me, a prisoner for His sake; but with the strength which comes from God bear your share of the hardship which the Gospel entails (2 Timothy 1:7-8).

THE EXAMPLE OF CHRISTIAN JOY IN MARRIAGE

This idea of Christian joy in suffering and sacrifice was beautifully expressed in the Church's former *Ritual of Marriage*. It contained the traditional "Exhortation Before Marriage," which at one time was standard reading to each couple at their wedding ceremony. It served as a witness to the Catholic Church's understanding of marriage and was a great inspiration to the young bride and groom.[6]

The exhortation began by reminding the young couple that they were entering into the union of marriage which is "most sacred and most serious," both because it was established by God and because it bound their lives together inseparably. As God intended, marriage required a complete and unreserved giving of self. In making marriage a Sacrament, Jesus wanted couples to base their love for each other on the example of His own self-sacrificing love. This love led Him to give Himself for His Mystical Spouse, the Church, by shedding His Blood for our Redemption.

The young couple, starry-eyed on their wedding day, might easily think it will be all wine and roses, and they will "live happily ever after." But this only happens in fairy tales and Hollywood movies. (As an old priest I knew used to say, "Love is blind, but marriage is the eye-opener.") So the exhortation offers a point of definite realism:

> This union, then, is most serious, because it will bind you together for life in a relationship so close and so intimate, that it will profoundly influence your whole future. That

---

[6] As an altar boy I served many weddings. I remember hearing this exhortation over and over again, and its inspiring message made a deep impression on me.

future, with its hopes and its disappointments, its successes and its failures, its pleasures and its pains, its joys and its sorrows, is hidden from your eyes. You know that these elements are mingled in every life and are to be expected in your own. And so, not knowing what is before you, you take each other for better or for worse, for richer or for poorer, in sickness and in health until death.

What the exhortation says here is that the realistic expectation of future joys and sorrows requires that the couple have a total unconditional love for each other. This is truly a love of abandonment, "for better or for worse." Such love alone will enable the young couple to get through the ups and downs of daily life. The exhortation acknowledges this fact as it continues:

Truly, then, these words (your wedding vows) are most serious. It is a beautiful tribute to your undoubted faith in each other, that, recognizing their full import, you are nevertheless so willing and ready to pronounce them.

The exhortation then points out the secret needed to find true happiness in married life: the willingness to sacrifice oneself for those one loves. In marriage, husband and wife share a "deeper and wider life. . . in common." Finally, in very striking words, we come to that joy which is found in sacrifices made out of love:

Henceforth, you belong entirely to each other; you will be one in mind, one in heart, and one in affections. And whatever sacrifices you may hereafter be required to make to preserve this common life, always make them generously. Sacrifice is usually difficult and irksome. Only love can make it easy; and perfect love can make it a joy. We are willing to give in proportion as we love. And when love is perfect, the sacrifice is complete.

Here we see again that the motive of love can make sacrifice and suffering easy, even a joy. As St. Augustine said many centuries ago, "There are no labors too difficult for loving hearts."

STEP FIVE: PERFECT JOY

The fifth and final attitude of a Christian toward suffering and the Cross is "perfect joy." This is truly the "ultra" level of virtue because it contains the fullest understanding of the secret power and beauty of the Cross. This is the farthest anyone can journey in the Christian life on this earth. "Perfect joy" is characteristic of those who have reached the summit of the spiritual life in the fullness of the Unitive stage. Only the Beatific Vision, which the saints enjoy in Heaven, lies beyond this stage.

Like the "joy in suffering" we have just been considering, "perfect joy" builds on the attitude of "abandonment" and brings it to completion. We can express the difference in these three attitudes in terms of a gradual intensification or expansion. The person who is "abandoned" is open to suffering and the Cross but may yet bear it with reluctance. The person who has "joy in suffering" is not only open to suffering but accepts it trustingly and courageously when it comes. The person at the level of "perfect joy" actually seeks for suffering or longs for it as the source of enormous graces and blessings and undergoes it gratefully and cheerfully.

Although not too many Christians reach this final level of virtue, it is useful for us to reflect upon its meaning. A relatively few deeply generous and faithful individuals have reached it.[7]

---

[7] The spiritual classic, *The Imitation of Christ*, sums this up in a chapter entitled, "The Small Number of the Lovers of the Cross of Jesus":

> Jesus has now many lovers of His heavenly kingdom, but few that are willing to bear His Cross.
>
> He has many that are desirous of comfort, but few of tribulation.
>
> He finds many companions of His table, but few of His abstinence.
>
> All desire to rejoice with Him, few are willing to suffer with Him.
>
> Many follow Jesus to the breaking of bread, but few to the drinking of the chalice of His passion.
>
> Many reverence His miracles, but few follow the ignominy of His Cross.
>
> Many love Jesus as long as they meet with no adversity.
>
> Many praise Him and bless Him as long as they receive consolation from Him.

THE APOSTLES AND "PERFECT JOY"

The Apostles reached the point of "perfect joy." Let us look at some examples of this attitude of "perfect joy" in regard to three things: first, their general desire to suffer for Jesus; second, their desire for humiliation; and third, their desire for martyrdom.

Despite our lack of details about the lives and activities of most of the Apostles after Pentecost, we can safely assume that their attitude toward suffering and the Cross matured into "perfect love." We have seen in the previous level of virtue how the Apostles had already overcome all fear. They rejoiced in being found worthy to suffer for the sake of Jesus and the spread of His Church. Under the light of the Spirit of Truth, Who would recall Jesus' words to them (John 14:26), they understood fully that when persecution came, it was a cause for great rejoicing. Had not the Lord told them this?

> Blest are you when they insult you and persecute you and utter every kind of slander against you because of Me. Be glad and rejoice, for your reward is great in Heaven; they persecuted the prophets before you in the very same way (Matthew 5:11-12).

We find clear evidence in Sacred Scripture and in different traditions that have come down to us of the desire of various Apostles to suffer for Jesus.

But if Jesus hides Himself and leaves them for a little while, they either fall into complaints or excessive dejection.

But they that love Jesus for Jesus' sake and not for any comfort of their own, bless Him no less in tribulation and anguish of heart than in the greatest consolation.

And if He should never give them His comfort, yet would they always praise Him and always give Him thanks.

Oh, how much is the pure love of Jesus able to do when it is not mixed with any self-interest or self-love. (Book II, Chapter 11, Confraternity of the Precious Blood, Brooklyn, New York, 1954, pp. 141-142)

We find this generous and loving attitude among the Apostles.

The Apostle St. Peter

First, we have the witness of St. Peter. He certainly loved Our Lord, and even though he was weak on Holy Thursday night, he proclaimed at the Last Supper his desire to suffer and die with Jesus (John 13:37). Many years later, he declared that Jesus suffered for our sakes in order to help us by His example to suffer for Him:

> When a man can suffer injustice and endure hardship through his awareness of God's presence, this is the work of grace in him. It was for this you were called, since Christ suffered for you in just this way and left you an example, to have you follow in His footsteps (1 Peter 2:19, 21).

St. Peter put his own teaching into practice throughout his life and endured many sufferings and hardships for the sake of Jesus. He suffered imprisonment in Jerusalem under King Herod Agrippa, but he was miraculously freed by an angel. He fearlessly continued to preach Christ openly in the city (Acts 12) at the risk of further suffering. Our Lord had foretold to him that he would climax his life of service feeding the lambs and sheep of His flock by the sacrifice of a martyr's death. St. John records Our Lord's prediction to St. Peter and then adds his own commentary:

> I tell you solemnly: as a young man you fastened your belt and went about as you pleased; but when you are older you will stretch out your hands and another will tie you fast and carry you off against your will. (What He said indicated the sort of death by which Peter was to glorify God.) (John 21:18-19).

This prediction of Our Lord was fulfilled in Rome in about the year 64 A.D. St. Peter was crucified (upside down according to tradition) under Emperor Nero in his gardens at the foot of the Vatican Hill (near to where St. Peter's Basilica stands today).

The Apostle St. Paul

Next, we look at St. Paul, the Apostle whose desire for suffering we know best of all. Right from the time Our Lord called him on the road to Damascus, Saul of Tarsus had a clear warning that as Paul the Apostle he was going to suffer. Our Lord had told Ananias, the man He sent to baptize Saul:

> This man (St. Paul) is the instrument I have chosen to bring My Name to the Gentiles and their kings and to the people of Israel. I Myself shall indicate to him how much he will have to suffer for My Name (Acts 9:15-16).

And suffer he did! In one of the most stirring sections of all his letters, he tells us of his many trials and sufferings as an Apostle. He endured them most willingly, because he was motivated by a tremendous love for Christ and for the salvation of others. He writes in a manner he calls "boasting with absolute foolishness":

> Now I am really talking like a fool — I am more: with my many labors and imprisonments, with far worse beatings and frequent brushes with death. Five times at the hands of the Jews I received forty lashes less one; three times I was beaten with rods; I was stoned once, shipwrecked three times; I passed a day and a night on the sea. I traveled continually, endangered by floods, robbers, my own people, the Gentiles; imperiled in the city, in the desert, at sea, by false brothers; enduring labor, hardship, many sleepless nights; in hunger and thirst and frequent fastings, in cold and nakedness. Leaving other sufferings unmentioned, there is that daily tension pressing on me, my anxiety for all the churches (2 Corinthians 11:23-28).

Furthermore, St. Paul frequently exhorted believers to be ready and willing to bear the Cross. For example, he told some of his earliest converts on his first missionary journey:

We must undergo many trials if we are to enter into the
reign of God (Acts 14:22).

Later, he encouraged St. Timothy (and through him, all of us)
to be ready to suffer willingly for the cause of Christ:

I remind you to stir into flame the Gift of God bestowed
when my hands were laid on you. The Spirit God has given
us is no cowardly spirit. . . With the strength which comes
from God bear your share of the hardship which the Gospel
entails. . . Bear hardship along with me as a good soldier of
Christ Jesus (2 Timothy 1:6-8; 2:3).

This fearless soldier of Christ valiantly fought the good fight
to the end. Like St. Peter, he also gave his supreme witness to Christ
by martyrdom for His sake. According to an ancient tradition, he
was martyred toward the end of the reign of the Emperor Nero,
possibly on the same day as St. Peter. He was beheaded by the sword
in a place near Rome now called the "Tre Fontane" ("The Three
Fountains"). The Basilica in Rome that bears his name is also his
burial place.

The Apostle St. Andrew

St. Andrew is another Apostle known for his great love of the
Cross and a great desire to suffer for Jesus. According to an account
found in a Medieval narrative, St. Andrew was crucified at Patras
in Greece. It is said that he was not nailed to the cross, but bound
to it by ropes. As a result, he remained alive on the cross for two
days. All the while he suffered, he also preached to the people.
According to another tradition, his cross was of the kind called
"saltire" or "decussate" (X-shaped).

According to the narrative, St. Andrew was condemned to
death by crucifixion for refusing to offer sacrifices to pagan idols.
When the pagan official, Aegeas, had the Apostle thrown into
prison, the people who greatly admired the saint could easily have

rioted to free him. However, St. Andrew personally calmed the mob and entreated the people earnestly not to riot, so that he could finally attain his ardently desired crown of martyrdom. As St. Andrew was led out to the place of martyrdom and saw the cross from a distance, he cried out:

> O good Cross, so long desired and now set up for my longing soul! . . . Hail, beloved Cross, consecrated by the Body of Christ, adorned by His members as with precious gems! . . . Confident and rejoicing I come to you; exultantly receive me, a disciple of Him Who hung on you. . . O Lord, King of eternal glory, accept me hanging on the Cross! (*The Church's Year of Grace*, Vol. 5, ed. by Dr. Pius Parsch, The Liturgical Press, Collegeville, 1958, p. 386)

THE APOSTLES' DESIRE TO BE HUMILIATED FOR LOVE OF JESUS

Another indication of the "perfect joy" of the Apostles was their readiness to suffer humiliation for Jesus. We have already seen evidence of this when they were whipped before the Sanhedrin for witnessing to Christ. St. Luke, the author of the Acts of the Apostles, tells us (5:41) that the Apostles were "full of joy" as a result of their scourging. The reason for such great joy was their awareness that "they had been worthy of ill-treatment for the sake of the Name." It is significant that "ill-treatment" implies not only the physical pain of the whipping, but the indignity and humiliation that accompanied it.

St. Paul summed up this aspect of bearing humiliations for the sake of Christ by saying that the Apostles have been made "fools for Christ":

> As I see it, God has put us Apostles at the end of the line, like men doomed to die in the arena. We have become a spectacle to the universe, to angels and men alike. We are

fools on Christ's account... We are the weak ones... They sneer at us! Up to this very hour we go hungry and thirsty, poorly clad, roughly treated, wandering about homeless. We work hard at manual labor. When we are insulted we respond with a blessing. Persecution comes our way; we bear it patiently. We are slandered, and we try conciliation. We have become the world's refuse, the scum of all; that is the present state of affairs (1 Corinthians 4:9-13).

Our Lord Himself was described by the prophet Isaiah as Someone Who, lacking all attractiveness and being held in disregard, would be spurned and avoided by others (Isaiah 53:2-3). The Apostles, in their ardent love for their Lord and Master, and in their striving to imitate Him in all things, must surely have desired a similar humiliation. No doubt they found it to be a source of the greatest joy to embrace what the saints have often called the "reproach" of the Cross for Jesus' sake.

The Apostles Desire Martyrdom

The third sign that the Apostles found "perfect joy" in their sufferings for Christ was their desire for the crown of martyrdom. Martyrdom is the giving up of our lives for our faith in Jesus and out of our love for Him. "Martyr" is actually the Greek word for "witness." The early Christians used it for those who shed their blood for Jesus because such an act of heroism was the greatest witness anyone could give to Jesus and their faith in Him.

It has traditionally been believed that all the Apostles, except St. John the Beloved, were put to death for the sake of Jesus and the preaching of His Gospel. In the early Church, martyrdom was the most coveted "crown of glory." Its blessing and graces were highly esteemed. By martyrdom, a person achieved the closest possible imitation of Christ. Furthermore, it was an opportunity to show the greatest love for God, since no greater love could be had than laying down one's life for the Lord. Finally, it assured those martyred of the reward of Heaven, because if they lost their life for Jesus, He told them they would certainly find it again (Matthew 16:25).

We have already seen the examples of the martyrdom of some of the Apostles, namely, St. Peter, St. Paul and St. Andrew. What of the others? The Acts of the Apostles tells us that *St. James the Greater*, brother of St. John, was the first of the Apostles to be martyred when he was beheaded in Jerusalem by King Herod Agrippa (Acts 12:1-2).

We have various traditions, understandably more or less complete, which inform us about the martyrdoms of the other Apostles. The second century Church historian, Hegesippus, wrote that *St. James the Less* was martyred by a group of Pharisees who threw him down from the pinnacle of the Jerusalem temple and then stoned him to death. *St. Thomas* went to India to spread the Gospel. He received his martyr's crown there by being speared to death near the city of Madras. *St. Philip* preached in Greece, and was crucified upside down at Hierapolis during the persecution of the Roman Emperor Domitian. *St. Bartholomew* (also called Nathaniel) travelled to Persia, India and finally Armenia, where he was flayed and beheaded by King Astyages. *St. Matthew* was said to have suffered martyrdom probably in Ethiopia. Western tradition holds that both *St. Simeon the Zealot* and *St. Jude Thaddeus* first went to preach in Egypt, and later to Persia where they were both martyred. *St. Matthias*, elected to replace Judas after his betrayal of Christ, was said to have preached in the area of the Caspian Sea. There he endured great persecution and was finally martyred. Even *St. John the Evangelist* was, according to the early Church writer Tertullian, sent to Rome during the persecution of the Emperor Domitian. There he miraculously escaped martyrdom by emerging unscathed from a cauldron of boiling oil. He was later exiled to the island of Patmos, where it is believed he wrote the Book of Revelation.

Our Lord Himself had been willing to endure the Cross and despise its shame for the sake of the joy which was set before Him (see Hebrews 12:1-3; 11-13). Would not the Apostles have kept their eyes fixed on Jesus as their example and their joy? This joy was the result of the Holy Spirit working in them after they had received Him in abundant measure at Pentecost. The Spirit had completely transformed them. He dispelled all their fears and gave them heroic courage. He allowed them to discover that what had previously seemed so difficult, even bitter and repulsive, in suffering actually had an attractiveness and joy out of love for God and for the salvation of others.

In summary, perhaps we can look to St. Paul to be a spokesman for all the Apostles. He points out that their very sufferings with Christ entitled them to share in His consolation, which the Spirit of Joy, Whom Jesus sent from the Father, continuously poured out on the Church:

> Praised be God, the Father of Our Lord Jesus Christ, the Father of mercies, and the God of all consolation! He comforts us in all our afflictions and thus enables us to comfort those who are in trouble with the same consolation we have received from Him. As we have shared much in the suffering of Christ, so through Christ do we share abundantly in His consolation. If we are afflicted, it is for your encouragement and salvation and when we are consoled it is for your consolation, so that you may endure patiently the same sufferings we endure. Our hope for you is firm because we know that just as you share in the sufferings, so you will share in the consolation (2 Corinthians 1:3-7).

CHAPTER VI

Perfect Joy Among the Saints

HAVING LOOKED AT THE EXAMPLES of "perfect joy" in the lives of the Apostles, we will now look at the lives of the saints to find further illustrations of this same joy. We will use the same three reflections of "perfect joy" for the saints as we did for the Apostles. These are: first, their general desire to suffer for Jesus; second, their desire for humiliation; and third, their desire for martyrdom.

THE SAINTS' DESIRE TO SUFFER FOR JESUS

St. Teresa of Avila was deeply convinced that she had to share in the sufferings of Our Lord if she wanted to be like Him. So she adopted as her motto: "To suffer or to die, preferably to suffer!" Suffering was by no means easy for her. There is the famous story of her experience crossing a stream. She fell into the water and became soaking wet. Climbing up out of the stream, she heard the voice of the Lord speak in her heart: "Teresa, do you see how I treat My friends?" Without a moments hesitation, St. Teresa replied: "Lord, if this is the way You treat Your friends, no wonder You have so few of them!"

She struggled with her crosses as we do with ours, and they were indeed many and burdensome for her. I once met a man on a pilgrimage who shared with me a stanza from one of the saint's less

81

known poems. He had come across this stanza in grammar school
and it made a lasting impression on him. In it St. Teresa candidly
expressed her dilemma regarding her sufferings. Translated from
the Spanish original, it reads:

> Neither with You nor without You
> are my sorrows comforted;
> with You, because You kill me,
> and without You, because I'm dying.

As St. Teresa puts it here, she realizes she has a choice: either
to remain with Jesus or to leave Him. If she chooses to remain with
Him, He will always have His Cross, and this means continual
suffering for her — "You kill me." But she has to choose this,
because the alternative, to leave Jesus, is even more painful — "I'm
dying." In other words, better to have Jesus and to suffer than to be
without Him and be in total anguish!

Why Did the Saints Desire to Suffer?

A threefold love for Jesus motivated the saints to desire
suffering.

Desire to Imitate Jesus

First, the saints had a loving desire to imitate Him, even in His
sufferings. From the earliest Christian centuries, the imitation of
Christ was regarded as the highest degree of holiness. But how could
a person faithfully imitate Our Lord, unless he also imitated Him in
His sufferings? St. Bernard of Clairvaux encouraged his own followers to strive for such a faithful imitation of the suffering Christ. He
argued that we who are the members of Christ's Mystical Body must
resemble Him Who is our Head:

It is not fitting that a head (Jesus) crowned with thorns should rest upon members which shrink from pain. The Master's body was bruised and broken; so let it then be with ours. Our souls will be only the more beautiful for having taken on this likeness of Christ. (Quoted by A. Tanquerey and L. Arand in *Doctrine and Devotion*, Desclee, Belgium, 1933, pp. 400-401).

Desire to Share in Jesus' Sufferings

Second, there was a loving desire to share in His sufferings. Love draws us to union with those we love. The Holy Spirit stirs up in those who love the Lord, particularly in the Unitive stage, a burning desire to be united with Him in His sufferings. Not only is this the supreme sign of being united with Jesus, but it is also the chief means of sharing in His sorrow in order to prepare to share in His joy. The only way to come to be with the Risen Lord in His Heavenly glory is to be associated with His earthly sufferings. To share briefly in Good Friday is to share unendingly in Easter Sunday. St. Paul reminds us of this:

> You can depend on this: If we have died with Him, we shall also live with Him; If we hold out to the end, we shall also reign with Him (2 Timothy 2:11-12).

The Example of St. Francis

St. Francis of Assisi is an example of someone who felt this remarkable desire to share Jesus' sufferings as much as he could. In 1224, about two years before his death, St. Francis was staying at a mountain solitude called Mount Alvernia where he was praying and fasting in preparation for the coming feast of St. Michael the Archangel on September 29. Francis always had a special devotion to the Prince of the Angels. While there, St. Francis received a premonition that he would share in Jesus' sufferings in a special way. We read the following description of how the Lord prepared him:

> In the hermitage chapel where Brother Leo (a priest-friar, who was also St. Francis' close friend and confessor) said Mass, St. Francis asked his friend to open the missal (which contained the Scripture readings) three times at random, and each time it opened at the story of the Passion. "By this sign," writes St. Bonaventure, "the Saint understood that, having imitated Christ in his life, he was also to imitate Him in the sufferings that preceded His death." So, filled with courage, despite his ruined health and physical exhaustion, he made ready for martyrdom. (Omer Englebert, O.F.M. *St. Francis of Assisi*, Ann Arbor, MI: Servant Publications, 1979, p. 242)

Finally, it was on or near the feast of the Exaltation of the Cross, September 14, 1224, that St. Francis was inspired to offer the Lord in prayer his desire to share His two-fold experience on the Cross:

> In that hour which precedes sunrise, kneeling before his hut, Francis prayed, his face turned toward the east. "O Lord, he pleaded, I beg of You two graces before I die — to experience in myself in all possible fullness the pains of Your cruel Passion, and to feel for You the same love that made You sacrifice Yourself for us." (*Ibid.*, p. 242)

The answer to St. Francis' prayer came in the form of the sacred stigmata. These were the marks of the five great wounds of Jesus on His Cross, the wounds of the nails in His hands and in His feet, as well as the wound in His side from the piercing by the Roman centurion's lance. These wounds became impressed into the hands, feet, and side of St. Francis. He had come to share both the suffering and the love that Jesus experienced on the Cross in a marvelously unique way!

Desire to Share in Jesus' Mission of Salvation

The third love for Jesus that prompted the saints to desire to suffer was to share in His mission of bringing all people to salvation. We can see an example of this love in the writings of St. *Therese of Lisieux*. She must have been filled with "perfect joy," so desirous was she to suffer to assist in the salvation and sanctification of others. She was not content to bear only her own sufferings; she wanted to be able to share the sufferings of Our Lord Himself and the sufferings of all the saints combined. She expresses her ardent desire in the following striking passage of her autobiography, *The Story of a Soul*:

> Above all, O my Beloved Savior, I would shed my blood for You even to the very last drop.
>
> Martyrdom was the dream of my youth and this dream has grown with me within Carmel's cloisters. But here again, I feel that my dream is a folly, for I cannot confine myself to desiring one kind of martyrdom. To satisfy me I need all. Like You, my Adorable Spouse, I would be scourged and crucified. I would die flayed like St. Bartholomew. I would be plunged into boiling oil like St. John; I would undergo all the tortures inflicted upon the martyrs. With St. Agnes and St. Cecilia, I would present my neck to the sword, and like Joan of Arc, my dear sister, I would whisper at the stake Your Name, O JESUS. When thinking of the torments which will be the lot of Christians at the time of Anti-Christ, I feel my heart leap with joy and I would that these torments be reserved for me. Jesus, Jesus! If I wanted to write all my desires, I would have to borrow Your Book of Life, for in it are reported all the actions of all the saints, and I would accomplish all of them for You. (*Story of a Soul: The Autobiography of St. Therese of Lisieux*, translated from the original manuscripts by John Clarke, O.C.D., ICS Publications, Washington, D.C., 1976, p. 193)

To many persons reading this quote, it may seem that no one in their right mind could ever possibly desire to suffer so much! One may well be tempted to regard this as "excessive exaggeration" or "pure fantasy." Yet we find a strand of similar thinking in the dying words of one of the great heroes of the American Revolution, Nathan Hale. Before being put to death by the British, he declared: "I have only one regret: that I have but one life to give for my country!" Now, if someone who is honored as a national hero could express this sentiment purely out of love for his country, could not a person desire to suffer again and again for the love of Jesus, the God-Man Who has loved us so much?

THE SAINTS' DESIRE TO BE HUMILIATED FOR THE LOVE OF JESUS

Just as the Apostles willingly and cheerfully endured the "reproach" of Christ and His Cross, so, too, the saints also embraced humiliations with "perfect joy" for the sake of Jesus. This intensified their imitation of Jesus and guaranteed them a greater share in His sufferings.[1]

---

[1] Accepting humiliations is certainly not easy. It seems to go entirely against the grain! We have our self-respect, our dignity, our sensitivities, and we demand that everyone acknowledge them. And woe to those who fail to do so! This is why the ability to accept humiliations joyfully is no small task. It demands a heroic level of virtue. But it also pays back a marvelous share in the consolation of Our Lord. In his *Exhortation to Martyrdom*, Origen, one of the early Church Fathers, writes on this point:

Now is the time for Christians to rejoice, since Scripture says that we should rejoice in our sufferings, knowing that suffering trains us to endure with patience, patient endurance makes us pleasing to God, and being pleasing to God gives us ground for a hope that will not be disappointed. Only let "the love of God be poured forth in our hearts through the Holy Spirit."

"The more we share in the sufferings of Christ, the more we share, through Him, in His consolation." We should be extremely eager to share in Christ's sufferings and to let them be multiplied in us if we desire the superabundant consolation that will be given to those who mourn. This consolation will not perhaps be the same for all, but if it were, Scripture would not say: "The more we share in the sufferings of Christ, the more we share in His consolation." Sharing in His consolation will be proportionate to our sharing in His suffering. We learn this

The spiritual writer, Father Olier, teaches that there are three degrees of humility.

The first degree is when we are able to rejoice in the knowledge of our own faults and shortcomings. We can acknowledge that, even when we have done all that we should, we are still only "useless" or "unprofitable" servants, as Our Lord reminds us in the Gospel (Luke 17:10). Like St. Paul, we learn to glory in our weaknesses so that the power of Christ may be with us (2 Corinthians 12:9). It takes a great deal of honesty and integrity to admit candidly to ourselves our own faults and sins. This means that we do not try to cover them up or justify them by rationalizing them away in our own minds. Although this kind of honesty can be very painful to our pride and vanity, it can free us from many obsessive thoughts and compulsive forms of "perfectionism."

The second degree of humility is the desire to want our faults and shortcomings — in general, our "uselessness" — to be known by others. It is one thing to admit our faults to ourselves, but it is quite another thing for someone else to dare to admit them to us! In front of others we are tempted to resort to all kinds of excuses and rationalizations to show that we really do not have any faults, or at least that we are not nearly as bad as some other people are. If we are truly humble, however, we realize that to be true to ourselves, we must likewise be true to others. The humble person never tries to be one thing in front of people and another thing behind their backs. We cannot have virtues that are only skin deep, used merely to impress others or to advance our own cause for self-canonization!

St. Francis of Assisi is an example of someone who genuinely welcomed the honesty of others, even when it served to humble him. He accepted any admonition or rebuke without anger or offense. An early biographer of his, Thomas of Celano, preserved an incident that illustrates this clearly. St. Francis was riding a

---

from one (St. Paul) who could say with all confidence: "We know that as you share in the sufferings, so you will share in the consolation as well." (N. 41-42: PG 11, 618-619) in *The Liturgy of the Hours*, Vol. II, pp. 1858-1859)

donkey through a field owned by a peasant. The peasant, who was working in the field at the time, asked the saint if he was the Brother Francis everyone talked about:

> When the man of God humbly replied that he was the man he (the peasant) was asking about, the peasant said, "Try to be as good as you are said to be by all men, for many put their trust in you. Therefore I admonish you never to be other than you are expected to be." But when the man of God Francis heard this, he got down and threw himself before the peasant and humbly kissed his feet, thanking him for being kind enough to give him this admonition. Since therefore he was so famous as to be thought a saint by many, he considered himself lowly before God and men, neither did he feel any pride over his wide-spread fame or over his sanctity. (*Second Life* by Thomas of Celano, Ch. 111, par. 142 in *Omnibus*, p. 477)

Now if this second degree of humility seems so impossible, what about the third degree? This last and highest degree of humility, according to Father Olier, is to desire to be treated as useless. It is to desire humiliation for the sake of Jesus Who was humiliated. Often humble persons are keenly aware of their faults but other people hardly take notice of them because these short-comings are usually so insignificant. Humble persons desire to be treated according to what they believe their faults and shortcomings and general "uselessness" deserve. Truly humble persons fear praises that could make them proud; rather, they relish scorn as a way of keeping from pride and arrogance.

Again we can turn to St. Francis who possessed this degree of virtue. St. Bonaventure describes the attitude of the little poor man of Assisi:

> Therefore as Christ's true disciple, he was careful to pre-serve a low (humble) opinion of himself and appear worth-less in the eyes of others, keeping in mind the words of the

Supreme Teacher: "What is highly esteemed among men is an abomination in God's sight" (Luke 16:15). He often used to remark: "What a man is before God, that he is and no more." Consequently he was convinced that it was foolish to be elated when people showed him marks of respect; he was upset by praise, but overjoyed when he was insulted. He liked to have people scorn him — that spurred him on to do better — and he hated to be praised, which could lead to a fall (into pride). (*The Major Life*, by St. Bonaventure, Ch. VI, par. 1, in *Omnibus*, p. 671)

The key to a proper understanding of these different degrees, especially of the second and third that involve other people, is the element of "desire" on the part of the person growing in humility. Because of the "reproach" Our Lord endured, truly humble people are drawn to want to imitate Him in the humiliations of His life and death. They long to share in them by the humiliations they themselves undergo in their own lives.

It must be pointed out, however, that in reality these people often enjoyed great acceptance and praise from their contemporaries, as we saw was the case with St. Francis. Yet, this adulation and praise did not destroy their humility. Rather, the essential ingredient of their humility was their "desire" to suffer reproach for the love of Jesus. This "desire," which was by no means a natural sentiment, safeguarded them against the sin of pride. It was a special grace of the Holy Spirit in the person's life. It was the culmination of a loving and joyful longing for Jesus, stirred up and strengthened in them by the inspiration of the Holy Spirit.

St. Francis' Teaching on "Perfect Joy"

One more example from the life of St. Francis shows how this desire for reproach is one of the supreme gifts of the Holy Spirit and a source of "perfect joy." This example is taken from a popular collection of stories known as *The Little Flowers of St. Francis* and is contained in a chapter entitled, "How St. Francis Taught Brother Leo That Perfect Joy Is Only In The Cross."

St. Francis was with one of his early companions, Brother Leo. Brother Leo, whom St. Francis affectionately called his "little lamb of God,"[2] was his priest-confessor. He was also the saint's frequent companion on his travels, especially in his later life. On a bitterly cold winter day, St. Francis and Brother Leo were walking from the Italian city of Perugia to the little Chapel of St. Mary of the Angels, located in the valley just below Assisi. Brother Leo was walking a short distance ahead of St. Francis. There was a mixture of rain, snow and sleet falling steadily down on them as they trudged along the path. All of a sudden, St. Francis, beginning to share with him the wisdom of the Holy Spirit, called out to Brother Leo:

> Brother Leo, even if the Friars Minor (Franciscan Friars) in every country give a great example of holiness and integrity and good edification, nevertheless, write down and note carefully that perfect joy is not in that. (*The Little Flowers of St. Francis*, Ch. 8, in *Omnibus*, p. 1318)

Brother Leo, who must have been startled by the suddenness of the saint's remark and equally surprised by what he had said, made no response. The two cold and hungry friars simply kept walking along silently in the rain, cold and sleet. Then all of a sudden, St. Francis cried out again in a strong voice:

> Brother Leo, even if a Friar Minor gives sight to the blind, heals the paralyzed, drives out devils, gives hearing back to the deaf, makes the lame walk, and restores speech to the dumb, and what is still more, brings back to life a man who has been dead four days, write that perfect joy is not in that. (*Ibid.*, p. 1318)

---

[2] Actually, "leo" in Latin means "lion." By calling him a "lamb," St. Francis was making a humorous contrast!

Still, no response from Brother Leo! But between long pauses of silence while trudging through the rain, St. Francis kept giving examples of what "perfect joy" was not:

> Brother Leo, if a Friar Minor knew all languages and all sciences and Scripture. . . and the secrets of consciences. . . (or) could speak with the voice of an angel. . . (or) preach so well that he should convert all infidels to the faith of Christ. . . write down and note carefully that perfect joy is not in that. (*Ibid.*, pp. 1318-1319)

Finally, Brother Leo, giving in to the suspense of St. Francis lesson, broke his silence:

> Now when he had been talking this way for a distance of two miles, Brother Leo in great amazement asked him: "Father, I beg you in God's Name to tell me where perfect joy is." (*Ibid.*, p. 1319)

St. Francis gave — with utter simplicity and vivid, concrete imagery — the most profound explanation of "perfect joy." He presented it in a way that only one who had become a "fool for Christ" could possibly begin to appreciate:

> When we come to St. Mary of the Angels, soaked by the rain and frozen by the cold, all soiled with mud and suffering from hunger, and we ring at the gate of the place and the brother porter comes and says angrily: "Who are you?" And we say, "We are two of your brothers." And he contradicts us, saying: "You are not telling the truth. Rather you are two rascals who go around deceiving people and stealing what they give to the poor. Go away!" And he does not open for us, but makes us stand outside in the snow and rain, cold and hungry, until night falls — then if we endure all those insults and cruel rebuffs patiently, without being troubled and without complaining, and if we reflect

humbly and charitably that that porter really knows us and that God makes him speak against us, oh, Brother Leo, write that perfect joy is there!

And if we continue to knock, and the porter comes out in anger, and drives us away with curses and hard blows like bothersome scoundrels, saying: "Get away from here, you dirty thieves. Who do you think you are? You certainly won't eat or sleep here!" And if we bear it patiently and take the insults with joy and love in our hearts, oh, Brother Leo, write that that is perfect joy!

And if later, suffering intensely from hunger and the painful cold, with night falling, we still knock and call, and crying loudly beg them to open for us and let us come in for the love of God, and he grows still more angry and says: "Those fellows are bold and shameless ruffians. I'll give them what they deserve!" And he comes out with a knotty club and grasping us by the cowl throws us onto the ground, rolling us in the mud and snow, and beats us with that club. If we endure all those evils and insults and blows with joy and patience, reflecting that we must accept and bear the sufferings of the Blessed Christ patiently for love of Him, oh, Brother Leo, write: that is perfect joy! (*Ibid*, pp. 1319-1320)

I do not know whether any other saint has ever given anything even slightly resembling this description of "perfect joy." As people read it, one can only imagine what their reaction will be. A priest-friend of mine, holding a meeting with some of his young parishioners, once read this story of St. Francis and perfect joy. When he had finished, a young teenager walked up to him and said in perfect candor, "Father, I don't think I like that kind of joy!!!" I am sure most of us would prefer some other experience of joy, too.

St. Francis was trying to teach an important lesson to Brother Leo. He no doubt exaggerated details to heighten the contrast between humble suffering and perfect joy. It certainly produced a dramatic effect. But we must be careful not to dismiss the story simply as exaggeration. Although St. Francis taught the lesson in terms of what he was then experiencing on his journey — hunger and cold and the need for shelter — it was by no means just a story off the top of his head. Its main point came from the very depths of his heart. It was the conviction with which he lived every day of his life in his ardent love for Jesus. It was the expression of his total devotion to the God-Man, Jesus, Who had become poor and humble for his sake. It was his burning desire to imitate Him Who endured rejection and suffering for love of us. As St. Francis often reminded his friars, "Greatly to be loved is the love of Him Who has loved us so much!"

Remember, also, what has been said about the five stages of suffering, namely, that a person has to grow to understand and value each succeeding stage. For example, probably the proverbial "99.4%" of those who read St. Francis' story of "perfect joy" would find this description far too overwhelming. Now if we worked out this percentage in terms of 10,000 people who read it, that would mean that 9,940 readers would not relate very well, if at all, to St. Francis' idea of perfect joy. But that still leaves us with 60 other people. Maybe that small fraction of people are at the point where they can appreciate the impact of St. Francis' message! Some who have come to accept suffering with "abandonment" might be able to begin to grasp his teaching, while those in the stage of "joy in suffering" would much more readily appreciate this ideal. Others may still need to grow through the stages of "patience" and "resignation" to lead them to this same point. But all those who have reached the point of appreciating "perfect joy" — and granted they are relatively few in number, according to such spiritual authorities as St. Teresa of Avila and St. John of the Cross — can see it as a source of many blessings. This is why St. Francis concluded his teaching on "perfect joy" by pointing out that its source is the Holy Spirit:

And now hear the conclusion, Brother Leo. Above all the graces and gifts of the Holy Spirit which Christ gives to His friends is that of conquering oneself and willingly enduring sufferings, insults, humiliations, and hardships for the love of Christ. For we cannot glory in all those other marvelous gifts of God as they are not ours but God's as the Apostle Paul says: "What have you that you have not received?" (1 Corinthians 4:7). But we can glory in the Cross of tribulations and afflictions, because that is ours, and so the apostle says, "I will not glory save in the Cross of Our Lord Jesus Christ!" (Galatians 6:14). To Whom be honor and glory forever and ever. Amen. (*Ibid.*, p. 1320)

"Perfect joy" is indeed a very precious gift of the Holy Spirit. It makes us rejoice in sharing Jesus' humiliation because then we know we will come to share in His glorification. Those who die with Jesus will rise with Him. Those who suffer insult and rejection with Him will be glorified with Him. St. Peter tells us that when we suffer insult and humiliation because of our love for Jesus, then the Holy Spirit will be with us in His glory:

Do not be surprised, beloved, that a trial by fire is occurring in your midst. It is a test for you, but it should not catch you off guard. Rejoice instead, in the measure that you share Christ's sufferings. When His glory is revealed, you will rejoice exultantly. Happy are you when you are insulted for the sake of Christ, for then God's Spirit in its glory has come to rest on you (1 Peter 4:12-14).

There are many more examples we could give from the lives of the saints to illustrate their "perfect joy" in suffering humiliations for Jesus' sake. But this lesson from St. Francis' life serves to exemplify this quality for all the saints.

THE SAINTS' DESIRE TO SUFFER MARTYRDOM

Let us now turn to the third and final desire of the saints by which they expressed their "perfect joy" in suffering. This was their desire for martyrdom.

Jesus Himself became the "Supreme Martyr," witnessing to His love for us by giving His own life for us on the Cross. Now if Jesus was willing to become the first and greatest grain of wheat to die so that we as other grains of wheat might come to life (John 12:24), and if He, the Good Shepherd, was willing to lay down His life for all of us who are the sheep of His flock (John 10:11), the saints wanted to show Him their total love in return. This is why they could even go to their martyrdom cheerfully.

One consoling grace which the Holy Spirit bestowed on many of those who suffered martyrdom was the realization that they would not suffer alone. He sustained them with the inner conviction that Jesus would suffer in them. This conviction produced in them an unexplainable joy that remained even in the midst of some of the cruelest sufferings.

> In reading the history of the martyrs, we frequently find that if they did not fear to suffer, and that if they were happy in the midst of the most frightful tortures, it was only because they realized that Christ was suffering in them. We read, for instance, that St. Felicitas, being in the throes of childbirth shortly before she was put to death, cried aloud from pain. One of her jailers approached her and said: If you are unable now to bear this pain, what will you do when you face the wild beasts? She answered: Now it is I who suffer. But then another will come to me who will suffer for me, because I also shall suffer for Him. (Allard, "Historie des persecutions," t. II, p. 125, as quoted in *Doctrine and Devotion*, by A. Tanquerey and L. Arand, Desclee & Com., Tournai, Belgium, 1933, pp. 335-336)

The Example of St. Ignatius of Antioch

Among the early Christians, *St. Ignatius of Antioch* is one whose sentiments we know well regarding his coming martyrdom. His ardent desire to die for Jesus and thereby win the coveted crown of martyrdom is quite striking. He was bishop of the Church at Antioch in Syria.[3] He was condemned to death for his faith in Jesus during the persecution under the Roman Emperor Trajan around 107 A.D. He was sentenced to be put to death by being fed to the lions in the amphitheater at Rome. It is said that he joyfully submitted his limbs to the chains which would bind him as a prisoner until he got to Rome.

Enroute by ship from Antioch to Rome, St. Ignatius wrote seven letters which give us important information about life in the early Church. One of these letters was written to the Church community at Rome. He was afraid that these Christians would use their influence at the imperial court to have his life spared. His letter contains a heartfelt plea to them not to prevent him from going to the Lord Whom he loved so totally:

> I am writing to all the churches to let it be known that I will gladly die for God if only you do not stand in my way. I plead with you: show me no untimely kindness. Let me be food for the wild beasts, for they are my way to God. I am God's wheat and shall be ground by their teeth so that I may become Christ's pure bread. Pray to Christ for me that the animals will be the means of making me a sacrificial victim for God.
>
> No earthly pleasures, no kingdoms of this world can benefit me in any way. I prefer death in Christ Jesus to power over the farthest limits of the earth. He Who died in place of us is the one object of my quest. He Who rose for our sakes is my one desire. The time for my birth is close at hand.

---

[3] Some Church historians say he was the immediate successor of St. Peter as Bishop of Antioch; others say there was another bishop between St. Peter and St. Ignatius.

Forgive me, my brothers. Do not stand in the way of my birth to real life; do not wish me stillborn. My desire is to belong to God. Do not, then, hand me back to the world. Do not try to tempt me with material things. Let me attain pure light. Only on my arrival there can I be fully a human being. Give me the privilege of imitating the passion of my God. If you have him in your heart, you will understand what I wish. You will sympathize with me because you will know what urges me on. (*Letter to the Romans* by St. Ignatius of Antioch, Cap. 4, 1-2; 6, 1 ff., Funk 1, 217-223, as quoted in *The Liturgy of the Hours*, Catholic Book Publishing Co., New York, 1975, Vol. 4, pp. 1490-1491)

The compelling love and desire of this saintly martyr to give his all for Jesus are evident. He expresses this most beautifully in his image of being like wheat that will be ground down by the lions' teeth to form the flour of which he will be molded into the likeness of Christ and united with Him forever. Yet, despite his firm protest of readiness to die for Jesus, he must have had momentary doubts and temptations that in the face of death itself he might weaken in his resolve:

And supposing I should see you, if then I should beg you to intervene on my behalf, do not believe what I say. Believe instead what I am now writing to you. For though I am alive as I write to you, still my real desire is to die. My love of this life has been crucified, and there is no yearning in me for any earthly thing. Rather, within me is the Living Water which says deep inside me: "Come to the Father." (*Ibid.*, p. 1491)

The "Living Water" here is no doubt a reference to the Holy Spirit Who strengthened and encouraged St. Ignatius in his resolve to pass through death to the Father. It is this same Spirit Who sustained the joy and desire he had to suffer death, just as Our Lord Himself referred to His own death as a "baptism" He had to undergo

— a death He anguished over until it was accomplished (Luke 12:50). In a further statement, St. Ignatius reiterated once again how the Christians at Rome will prove to be his friends if they allow him to reach his heart's desire:

> Pray for me that I may obtain my desire. I have not written to you as a mere man would, but as one who knows the mind of God. If I am condemned to suffer, I will take it that you wish me well. If my case is postponed, I can only think that you wish me harm. (*Ibid.*, p. 1492)

The Example of St. John de Brebeuf

Let us take an example nearer to our own times of a saint who prepared himself for his death as a martyr with the expectation of "perfect joy." *St. John de Brebeuf* was one of eight Jesuit martyrs of North America who gave their lives for Christ between the years 1642 and 1649. St. John courageously suffered savage torture and death at the hands of the Iroquois on March 16, 1649. Even while being tortured, he was given the courage through the Holy Spirit to preach both to his persecutors and to his fellow Christian captives who were suffering along with him. A short time before his death, he recorded his feelings about his almost certain martyrdom in his spiritual diary:

> For two days now I have experienced a great desire to be a martyr and to endure all the torments the martyrs suffered.
>
> Jesus, my Lord and Savior, what can I give You in return for all the favors You have first conferred on me? I will take from Your hand the cup of Your sufferings and call on Your name. I vow before Your Eternal Father and the Holy Spirit, before Your Most Holy Mother, and her most chaste spouse, before the angels, apostles and martyrs, before my blessed fathers, Saint Ignatius and Saint Francis Xavier — in truth I vow to You, Jesus, my Savior, that as far as I have

the strength I will never fail to accept the grace of martyrdom, if some day You in Your infinite mercy should offer it
to me, Your most unworthy servant.

I bind myself in this way so that for the rest of my life I will
have neither permission nor freedom to refuse opportunities of dying and shedding my blood for You, unless at a
particular juncture I should consider it more suitable for
Your glory to act otherwise at that time. Further, I bind
myself to this so that, on receiving the blow of death, I shall
accept it from Your hands with the fullest delight and joy
of spirit. For this reason, my beloved Jesus, and because of
the surging joy which moves me, here and now, I offer my
blood and body and life. May I die only for You, if You will
grant me this grace, since You willingly died for me. Let me
so live that You may grant me the gift of such a happy
death. In this way, my God and Savior, I will take from
Your hand the cup of Your sufferings and call on Your
name: Jesus, Jesus, Jesus!

My God, it grieves me greatly that You are not known, that
in this savage wilderness all have not been converted to
You, that sin has not been driven from it. My God, even if
all the brutal tortures which prisoners in this region must
endure should fall on me, I offer myself most willingly to
them and I alone shall suffer them all. (From the "Spiritual
Diaries by St. John de Brebeuf," *The Jesuit Relations and
Allied Documents*, The Burrows Brothers Co., Cleveland,
1898, 164, 166 in *The Liturgy of the Hours*, Vol. 4, pp. 1503-
1504)

No doubt such generous love described by St. John de Brebeuf
could only spring from the Holy Spirit. The first fruit of His working
in us is love, even more so to such a heroic degree. Likewise, joy is
one of His fruits. Only the Holy Spirit could have led St. John de
Brebeuf to write that he would accept the blow that brought his
death "with the fullest delight and joy of spirit." The Holy Spirit

inspired in him the "surging joy" which led him to such a "great desire to be a martyr and endure all the torments the martyrs suffered." The "perfect joy" of the martyrs can only be understood in the light of an overwhelming grace of God.

In these last two chapters, we have traced the spiritual development of the Apostles and of some of the saints as they grew in deepening conversion to Our Lord. We have seen how their attitude toward the Cross changed from rejection to rejoicing, and how their level of virtue matured each step of the way. Our Lord Himself initiated the Apostles' spiritual development, and the Holy Spirit brought it to completion.

Now the challenge is ours. We must pass through a development similar to the Apostles. Our Lord will teach us many of the same truths He taught to the Apostles. He will confirm His teaching about the Cross with the example of His own life and death. He will also send us the Spirit of Joy from the Father to help us understand the great mysterious paradox of all Christian life: with Jesus all our sorrow will be turned into joy! We will come to know the truth expressed long ago by an unknown Christian author of the second century: "They are happy who, putting all their trust in the Cross, have plunged into the water of life!"

CHAPTER VII

The Joy of the Holy Spirit Springs from Love

T O UNDERSTAND FULLY HOW the Holy Spirit can turn suffering into joy, we must look at love, which ultimately motivates us to suffer and which alone produces joy. Many human experiences in life can only be explained because of the love behind them. For example, love alone can explain the often heroic actions of many mothers toward their children — as in times of sickness, misfortune, tragedy, and even death itself. Love alone can explain why sometimes for the sake of friendship, one is willing to sacrifice so much, even his or her own life. Love enables two friends to share one mind, one heart, one soul, in a sense, one life! Even more so, the love for God, the highest love of all, can produce still greater expressions of giving and consequently of rejoicing.

Love produces such results because its chief characteristic is that "love tends to give itself." This is how the philosophers of old described love. This giving of self is linked to an other quality of love expressed in the old saying: "Love is blind." This means that love often ignores any self-centered concerns. As another old saying puts it: "Love does not stop to count the cost." It simply tends to give as long as there is something to give. St. Paul marvelously described this characteristic of love:

> Love does not rejoice in what is wrong but rejoices with the truth. There is no limit to love's forbearance, to its trust, its hope, its power to endure (1 Corinthians 13:6-7).

Let us now look closely at how the Holy Spirit can use various motivations of love even in sacrifice and suffering, as the basis for the deepest spiritual joys.

FOUR REASONS FOR CHRISTIAN JOY IN SUFFERING

In general, love has four different reasons or motives for rejoicing in suffering, because there are four different blessings that such suffering can produce. These blessings are: (1) the glory and praise of God; (2) graces for our spiritual life; (3) rewards for eternal life; and (4) graces and blessings for others.

First Motive of Joy: The Glory and Praise of God

Suffering out of love can bring the joy of praising and glorifying God. By choosing to love and serve God above all created things, we give Him great honor and praise. When suffering tries our love by making it more difficult to choose God, then our actual decision to do so is an added honor and praise we give to Him. Since it enhances our love, it also enhances our giving, and consequently our praise.

We see an example of this when, to give him an opportunity to make up for his three denials of Him, Our Lord, after His Resurrection, asked St. Peter three times, "Do you love Me?" Once St. Peter reaffirmed his love and loyalty to Jesus, Our Lord added a prophecy about St. Peter's final imprisonment and death:

> I tell you solemnly, as a young man you fastened your belt and went about as you pleased; but when you are older you will stretch out your hands and another will tie you fast and carry you off against your will (John 21:18).

St. John the Evangelist comments on this:

What He said indicated the sort of death by which Peter was to glorify God (21:19).

Like his willingness to feed the lambs and sheep of Jesus' flock, St. Peter's willingness to suffer and even die was a sign of his love for the Lord and a means of giving Him glory. We too can rejoice in our own sufferings for they prove and perfect our love for God, thereby giving Him a greater praise and glory.

SECOND MOTIVE OF JOY: OBTAINING MANY GRACES FROM GOD

Suffering out of love also produces the joy of many graces for our spiritual life. Such suffering can greatly help our spiritual growth and development. We see this clearly in the letters of St. James and of St. Peter. Let us reflect briefly on each of them.

St. James enthusiastically stresses this point, writing about it in the very second line of his letter:

Count it pure joy when you are involved in every sort of trial. Realize that when your faith is tested this makes for endurance. Let endurance come to its perfection so that you may be fully mature and lacking in nothing (1:2-4).

Getting "involved in every sort of trial" applies in a special way to a person who reaches the Unitive stage in his spiritual growth. He characteristically passes through periods of trials that are generally more frequent and more intense than had been previously encountered. St. John of the Cross calls this period "the dark night of the spirit."

These trials are different than the earlier struggles in the spiritual life. For example, there were earlier efforts to practice various virtues, such as patience, or charity in thought and word. Furthermore, there were struggles to resist temptations of anger or lust, or to practice some mortification in our eating and drinking, or to persevere at prayer despite distractions and intervals of dryness.

The later trials of "the dark night of the spirit" are by comparison much longer and more intense. They often involve great trials of faith. A person may experience prolonged dryness in prayer, having no feeling of God's presence or action. He may be tormented by fears that God has even abandoned him. Because of his attempts to do good, there are often trials of being rejected by others. He may be misunderstood, misjudged, or criticized, despite acting with sincerity and honesty. Other trials may involve obsessive temptations that persist despite continued efforts to reject them, for they seem to be (and probably are) stirred up by the Devil himself. There may be trials of failure in one's undertakings, or of physical sufferings or even of tragedy.

In spite of all these profound sufferings, however, we can experience a very real spiritual joy following from these trials if we bear them out of love. Through them a person learns to overcome any final vestiges of self-centeredness and to focus on God with greater purity of heart. The blessings of such suffering in love are brought out clearly in the First Letter of St. Peter:

> There is cause for rejoicing here. You may for a time have to suffer the distress of many trials; but this is so that your faith, which is more precious than the passing splendor of fire-tried gold, may by its genuineness lead to praise, glory and honor when Jesus Christ appears. Although you have never seen Him, you love Him, and without seeing you now believe in Him, and rejoice with inexpressible joy touched with glory because you are achieving faith's goal, your salvation (1:6-9).

If we did not have our crosses in life, we would never be challenged to grow. Athletes, who must practice and discipline themselves by continuous strenuous effort, often say, "No pain, no gain." The trials of our spiritual lives are the "pain" that help us "gain" in holiness. No wonder those who deeply love God accept these trials joyfully.

We find this same teaching in the Letter to the Hebrews, where suffering is seen as a discipline for us. Just as our own parents disciplined us as best they could, so God does likewise for our eternal welfare:

> Endure your trials as the discipline of God, Who deals with you as sons. For what son is there whom his father does not discipline... At the time it is administered, all discipline seems a cause for grief and not for joy, but later it brings forth the fruit of peace and justice to those who are trained in its school (12:7, 11).

A person at this point of suffering is often comforted by the realization that these trials will cease in due time, once they have achieved the purpose for which God in His wisdom has allowed them. Then, as with a terrible storm, they will pass on, and tranquillity will return like the proverbial calm after the storm. The Holy Spirit will visit the soul, refreshing and renewing it with a deepened sense of peace and an abundance of His consolation and joy. St. Teresa of Avila always kept this conviction before herself in her famous bookmark:

> Let nothing disturb you,
> Nothing frighten you;
> All things are passing
> God never changes.
> Patient endurance attains to all things;
> Whoever possesses God is wanting in nothing;
> God alone suffices.

THIRD MOTIVE OF JOY: THE REWARD OF ETERNAL LIFE

The joy of knowing we will receive the rewards of eternal life is another motive for suffering out of love. We are motivated by these rewards with the hope that we shall come to possess the good things God has prepared for those who love Him (1 Corinthians 2:9). We find ourselves ardently striving to attain the merited crown that the Lord will award us if we, like St. Paul, persevere in fighting the good fight and running the race (2 Timothy 4:7-8). In a rather startling passage in the Letter to the Hebrews, we read that even Our Lord endured His sufferings for the "joy" of the rewards they would bring Him:

> Let us lay aside every encumbrance of sin which clings to us and persevere in running the race which lies ahead; let us keep our eyes fixed on Jesus Who inspires and perfects our faith. For the sake of the joy which lay before Him, He endured the Cross, heedless of its shame. He has taken His seat at the right of the throne of God. Remember how He endured the opposition of sinners; hence, do not grow despondent or abandon the struggle (12:1-3).

What was this "joy" set before Jesus? No doubt, it consisted of many elements. First of all, He knew that the humility and total obedience of His suffering and death would give the greatest possible honor and praise to His Heavenly Father, in reparation for the dishonor shown Him by the pride and disobedience of all the sins of mankind. Furthermore, in His great love for us He was also aware that by His sufferings He would win our salvation, snatching us away from eternal death and obtaining for us eternal life. Finally, He also knew it was according to the Father's will that through the shame of the Cross He would enter into His glory (Luke 24:26), and that He would be highly exalted and receive a Name above every other name and be proclaimed "Lord" by all (Philippians 2:8-11).

Hope Sustained the Joy of the Saints

The joy of suffering is always sustained by the virtue of hope. It is the hope we have of sharing in Jesus' glory and joy that makes our present sorrows bearable.

> I consider the sufferings of the present to be as nothing compared with the glory to be revealed in us. . . We ourselves, although we have the Spirit as first fruits, groan inwardly while we await the redemption of our bodies. In hope we were saved. But hope is not hope if its object is seen; how is it possible for one to hope for what he sees? And hoping for what we cannot see means awaiting it with patient endurance (Romans 8:18, 23-25).

The saints lived by this conviction. It was the driving force of their love and zeal. St. Paul shared this conviction with young Timothy, his disciple:

> You can depend on this: If we have died with Him we shall also live with Him; if we hold out to the end, we shall also reign with Him (2 Timothy 2:11-12).

St. Francis often exhorted his friars to remain steadfast in the service of the Lord. He encouraged them to be faithful to the vows they had made to God by referring to the promises God held out to them. At a famous general assembly of over three thousand of his friars in Assisi,[1] St. Francis urged them to persevere in God's service by contrasting the rewards and punishments of good and evil:

> We have promised great things and still greater have been promised to us. Let us keep the promises we have made; let us long for the fulfillment of those made to us. Pleasure is fleeting, but its punishment eternal. Suffering is light, but

---

[1] This famous general assembly of the friars was called the "Chapter of Mats" because the friars slept on mats in the open fields near the Chapel of St. Mary of Angels.

the glory to come is infinite. (*St. Francis of Assisi*, by Omer Englebert, O.F.M., Ann Arbor, MI: Servant Publications, 1979, p. 156)

One of the followers of St. Francis who took this message to heart was the Capuchin-Franciscan priest, St. Fidelis of Sigmaringen. Having lived a life dedicated to prayer and self-denial, and having spent his energy as a tireless preacher, his life was crowned with martyrdom for the Catholic Faith in Switzerland in 1622. In the last sermon he preached just a few days before his martyrdom, St. Fidelis revealed the source of his courage to suffer for Christ, namely, his faith and hope in the Resurrection:

> What was it that gave the holy apostles and martyrs the strength to endure severe trials and bitter sufferings? It was the (Catholic) Faith, especially faith in the Resurrection. What inspired the anchorites to renounce pleasure, to spurn honors, to trample riches underfoot and live a celibate life in the wilderness? It was the living Faith. What brings true followers of Christ today to put aside comfort, to abandon pleasures, to undertake what is hard and endure what demands sacrifice? It is the living faith that expresses itself through love. It is this faith that causes us to give up what is good here and now in the hope of what is to come, and to exchange what we have for what will be ours in the life to come. (*Elogium of St. Fidelis, Priest and Martyr* by Pope Benedict XIV)

A few days after he preached these words, St. Fidelis made this exchange in martyrdom, letting go of what he had in this life to obtain what would be his forever in eternal life.[2]

Many times we find the strength to persevere simply in the thought that if we remain faithful, the Lord will reward what we endure for His sake. It is important that we often reflect on eternal

---

[2] He was to become the proto-martyr both of the Capuchin-Franciscan Order and of the Sacred Congregation for the Propagation of the Faith.

life and what God has prepared for us. There is great consolation in the words of St. Paul:

> Eye has not seen, ear has not heard, nor has it so much as dawned on man what God has prepared for those who love Him! (1 Corinthians 2:9)

A final thought along this line is from a brief prayer of Cardinal Newman:

> Teach me, dear Lord, frequently and attentively to consider this truth: that if I gain the whole world and lose You, in the end I have lost everything; whereas if I lose this world and gain You, in the end I have lost nothing.

Who would not rejoice in being able to suffer for Christ when they realize that, in the end, they would have nothing to lose and everything to gain?

FOURTH MOTIVE OF JOY:
THE SALVATION AND SANCTIFICATION OF OTHERS

The fourth reason that suffering out of love can bring us joy is that it is the source of many graces and blessings for others. It is a characteristic of the kind of love Jesus taught us as "His own commandment" (John 15:12). Such Christ-like love is never limited to concern for one's own personal well-being. It must also extend to the well-being of our brothers and sisters in Christ, even for the least of them. This is especially true of concern for their ultimate well-being, their eternal salvation.[3]

---

[3] It has been said that the following is the greatest difference between a non-Christian mystic (e.g., a Buddhist or Hindu mystic) and a Christian mystic: The non-Christian mystic seeks such a total union with God that he is completely absorbed into Him like a drop of water falling into a great ocean; the Christian mystic seeks as close a union with God as possible (while yet retaining his own identity and individuality), but once he has attained such a unity with the Lord, he goes back and gets his brother and sister and brings them to Jesus also!

Joy in Working for the Salvation of Souls

Christians from the earliest times have been aware of the need to give themselves for the salvation and sanctification of others. This is called "zeal for the salvation of souls." It is generally one of the signs of authentic holiness. Did not such zeal and desire motivate Our Blessed Lord Himself? We express this thought in the Nicene Creed when we proclaim our belief that "for us and for our salvation He came down from Heaven." Our Lord Himself summed up His mission and the very purpose of His coming as the salvation of sinners:

> The Son of Man has come to search out and save what was lost (Luke 19:10).

Contrasting Himself to the "thieves" who came only to steal and slaughter and destroy the flock of the faithful sheep (John 10:10) and to the "hired hands" who flee for their own safety and abandon the flock in the face of danger (John 10:12), Jesus proclaims Himself a "true Shepherd" Who sacrifices Himself for the sake of the sheep whom He loves:

> I came that they might have life and have it to the full. I am the Good Shepherd; the Good Shepherd lays down His life for the sheep (John 10:10-11).

Joy in Heaven over one Repentant Sinner

Jesus stresses that when someone is saved from his sins and restored to God's love and to his place in God's household, the Church, there is always rejoicing. This is reflected clearly in Jesus' parables of mercy in Luke 15. For example, in the parable of the lost sheep, when the shepherd returns home after finding the lost sheep, carrying it on his own shoulders in jubilation:

> He invites friends and neighbors in and says to them: "Rejoice with me because I have found my lost sheep." I tell

you, there will likewise be more joy in Heaven over one repentant sinner than over ninety-nine righteous people who have no need to repent (Luke 15:6-7).

In another parable, Our Lord tells us about a woman who finds a silver piece she had lost. After searching the entire house, she finally finds it, and then she also rejoices:

She calls in her friends and neighbors to say, "Rejoice with me! I have found the silver piece I lost." I tell you, there will be the same kind of joy before the angels of God over one repentant sinner (Luke 15:9-10).

Finally, in a third parable, when a prodigal son returns home after a time of sinful living that nearly brought his life (and no doubt his father's) to the edge of despair, there is a celebration that, so to speak, "pulls out all the stops" — the finest clothes, music, dancing, and even killing the traditionally festive "fatted calf." The father explains to his older son the reason for such a joyous celebration:

We had to celebrate and rejoice! This brother of yours was dead, and has come back to life. He was lost and is found (Luke 15:32).

One of the joys of being a priest is to be able to hear the confession of someone whose life had been "lost in sin" and far from God but who now repents and returns to His love. The joy of giving absolution to such a penitent is one of the greatest consolations in the priestly ministry. Even though he is strictly bound to secrecy under the seal of Confession, the priest knows in his heart the profound joy of which Our Lord is speaking.

SUCH JOY INVOLVES THE CROSS

But attaining such joy often involves the Cross. Our Lord clearly teaches the relationship between the suffering of the Cross, and the salvation and sanctification of sinners. In His analogy of the grain of wheat He proclaims:

> I solemnly assure you, unless the grain of wheat falls to the earth and dies, it remains just a grain of wheat. But if it dies, it produces much fruit (John 12:24).

The "dying" of the grain of wheat is symbolic of the suffering of the Cross in a person's life. If the grain of wheat could choose, it would have two options: (1) remaining as it is, preserving itself intact in the protective security of its shell, enduring no pain of sacrifice or change, or (2) shedding its shell in the process of germination, surrendering the life-potential already present within its inner kernel and allowing itself to sprout into new stalks of grain, thus giving life to many new grains of wheat. Our Lord's point here is that there would be no new life for others, unless there was first a process of surrender and dying.

Jesus Himself would be the first and most important grain of wheat to surrender Himself and to die, thus giving life to others through His Cross. That is why He adds only a few verses later the effect of His saving death:

> I — once I am lifted up from earth — will draw all men to Myself. (This statement indicated the sort of death He had to die.) (John 12:32-33).

EXAMPLES OF THE SAINTS

St. Paul's Life of Joyous, Sacrificial Service

All those who would share in Jesus' work for the salvation of the world must become other grains of wheat falling to the earth and dying in the process of helping others come to life in the Spirit. St. Paul experienced this daily "dying" process in his work for the salvation of others. He looked upon himself as a "libation" or total offering, pouring himself out and spending himself for others (2 Timothy 4:6). He did not count the cost. He found his consolation in the converts he had made whom he would joyfully present to the Lord on the Day of His coming:

> As I look to the Day of Christ, you give me cause to boast that I did not run the race in vain or work to no purpose. Even if my life is to be poured out as a libation over the sacrificial service of your faith, I am glad of it and rejoice with all of you. May you be glad on the same score, and rejoice with me (Philippians 2:16-18).

For St. Paul, those whose salvation and sanctification he worked to attain would become his joy and his crown. So he spent himself willingly for them each day. He lists among all his sufferings as an Apostle, his concern for the numerous communities of converts and disciples he had established on his various missionary journeys:

> Leaving other sufferings unmentioned, there is that daily tension pressing on me, my anxiety for all the churches (2 Corinthians 11:28).

His concern for them was as tender as a mother's love; in fact, at certain times it was as painful as the pangs of labor in childbirth:

> You are my children, and you put me back in labor pains until Christ is formed in you (Galatians 4:19).

As an Apostle sharing in Christ's work of redemption, St. Paul saw that his own sufferings, when joined to those of Christ, had a redemptive value for others. He found joy in the spiritual good his sufferings could produce for the disciples he loved so much:

Even now I find my joy in the suffering I endure for you. In
my own flesh I fill up what is lacking in the sufferings of
Christ for the sake of His Body, the Church (Colossians
1:24).

The Joyful Zeal of St. Francis

All those who have loved God deeply over the centuries have
felt this same zealous desire to spend themselves for souls. One such
person was St. Francis. His zeal for the salvation of others played a
major part in one of the greatest trials he experienced. St. Francis
was at one time torn between two attractive choices.[4] On the one
hand, he was drawn toward going completely into solitude through
a life of total prayer and contemplation; on the other hand, he
wanted to remain among the people, going about preaching. He felt
he had received the gift of prayer rather than the gift of preaching.
He was personally attracted to a life of solitude because it allowed
him to live in a more constant union of prayer with God. Furthermore, a life of contemplation seemed to him to be favored with
more graces, and would lead to a greater purity of heart and practice
of virtue. In addition, he felt that through preaching, for which he
judged himself ill-suited because of his lack of education and

---

[4] This was not unlike a trial St. Paul himself had gone through. The great Apostle was
torn in two directions at once. On the one hand, he yearned to be united to Christ in
death. This he considered to be for his greater good. On the other hand, he wanted to
continue in this life so that he could help his converts and disciples grow further in
holiness in their new life in Christ. St. Paul had the heart of a dedicated shepherd; in
no way did he want to abandon his sheep. He wrote of his experience candidly in his
letter to his beloved Philippians:

I have full confidence that now as always Christ will be exalted through me,
whether I live or die. For, to me, "life" means Christ; hence dying is so much
gain. If, on the other hand, I am to go on living in the flesh, that means
productive toil for me — and I do not know which to prefer. I am strongly
attracted by both: I long to be freed from this life and to be with Christ, for that
is the far better thing; yet it is more urgent that I remain alive for your sakes. This
fills me with confidence that I will stay with you and persevere with you all for
your joy and your progress in the faith (Philippians 1:20-25).

experience in public speaking, he would have to become involved in many distractions and in a lessening of religious fervor.

Yet, for St. Francis there was one final thought he had to consider. Despite all the advantages of a life of prayer and the seeming disadvantages of preaching, there was one consideration that outweighed all the others in favor of his continuing to preach: it was the example of Jesus' own preaching and His desire to save all. St. Bonaventure tells us how St. Francis put it:

> There is one argument which seems to count more than all the rest in God's eyes and it is this: the only-begotten Son of God, Who is Wisdom itself, came down from the Father's embrace to save souls. He wanted to teach the world by His own example and bring a message of salvation to men whom He had redeemed at the price of His Precious Blood, washing them clean in It. . . He kept nothing for Himself, but generously surrendered all for our salvation. We are bound to act always according to the model which has been set before us in Him as on some high mountain; and so it seems that it is more in accordance with God's will that I should renounce the peace of contemplation and go out to work. (*The Major Life*, Ch. XII, par. 1, in *Omnibus*, p. 721)

Later, St. Francis sought confirmation of his decision through the prayerful discernment of Brother Silvester, a friar known for his deep prayer-life and the gift of prophecy, as well as that of St. Clare and her Sisters. Both assured him that the gifts with which he was so favored by God were not for himself alone, but were to be shared with all the people of God:

> By the inspiration of the Holy Spirit, Brother Silvester and St. Clare both came to the same conclusion. It was God's will that Francis should go out to preach as a herald of Christ. (*The Major Life*, Ch. XII, par. 2, in *ibid.*, p. 722)

St. Bonaventure wrote that St. Francis' concern for souls was the driving force in his efforts to win sinners for Christ, both by his prayers and good example:

> The fervor of Francis' love united him so closely to God that his heartfelt compassion was enlarged so as to embrace all those who shared the same gifts of nature and of grace as he. His tender love made him the brother of all creatures, and so it is no wonder that the love of Christ should unite him even more closely with those who bear the image of their Maker and are redeemed by the Blood of their Creator. He would not think himself Christ's lover, if he did not compassionate the souls whom He (Jesus) redeemed. He used to say that nothing should take precedence over the salvation of souls, because it was for souls that the only begotten Son of God hung upon the Cross. It was for souls that he (St. Francis) wrestled in prayer, for souls that he was so active in preaching, and it was for them that he went beyond all limits in giving good example. (*The Major Life*, Ch. IX, par. 4, *Ibid.* p. 700)

The Joyful Sacrifice of Other Saintly Persons

We could mention countless other saintly people for whom the salvation of souls was the driving force of their lives. Let it suffice to mention just a few examples.

St. Catherine of Siena

This great saint spent a number of years in relative solitude, leading a life of intense contemplative prayer. Moved by her great love for God toward an overwhelming love of her neighbor, she abandoned her life of tranquility to an intense apostolate. She worked untiringly and heroically for reform in the Church, reaching even to the Pope himself. She summed up her apostolic zeal when she said: "I would be willing to work in the mouth of hell for the salvation of souls!"

St. John Bosco

The motto of St. John Bosco, who possessed untiring energy and zeal for the spiritual welfare of youth, was: "Give me souls and take all the rest!"

St. Therese of Lisieux

Then there is the example of St. Therese of Lisieux, whose life was characterized by hidden prayer and sacrifice for the conversion of sinners. She began at the age of twelve, praying for a hardened criminal. Although condemned to death, he refused to see a priest or receive the Sacraments of the Church. Young Therese prayed and offered sacrifices for his conversion; she then asked God for a "sign" that He accepted her efforts. She received it when she read in a newspaper an account of his execution which stated that the criminal, though still refusing a priest, reached up at the very last moment to kiss a crucifix which hung near him.

We find evidence of her burning desire for the salvation of souls throughout her whole life. In one place, she writes of her life that she has "come to save souls and above all to pray for priests." At another time she states:

> There is only one thing to do during the night of this life, and that is to love Jesus with all the strength of our hearts, and to save souls for Him so that He will be loved.

Perhaps the most vivid expression of her zeal for souls was reflected in her burning desire to be a worldwide missionary. She expresses this in a prayer in her autobiography:

> Ah! in spite of my littleness, I would like to enlighten souls as did the Prophets and the Doctors. I have the vocation of the Apostle. I would like to travel over the whole earth to preach Your Name and to plant Your glorious Cross on infidel soil. But O my Beloved, one mission alone would

not be sufficient for me, I would want to preach the Gospel on all the five continents simultaneously and even to the most remote isles. I would be a missionary, not for a few years only but from the beginning of creation until the consummation of the ages. But above all, O my Beloved Savior, I would shed my blood for You even to the very last drop. (*Story of a Soul: The Autobiography of St. Therese of Lisieux*, translated by John Clarke, O.C.D., ICS Publications, Institute of Carmelite Studies, Washington, D.C., 1976, pp. 192-193)

Even at the time of her death, this saint of the "little way" was determined to "spend her Heaven doing good upon earth" and to "let fall from Heaven a shower of roses till the end of time."

Mother Teresa of Calcutta

In our own day, we have an inspiring example of zealous apostolic work and prayer in Mother Teresa of Calcutta. In every chapel of her Missionaries of Charity, you will always find the words of Our Lord on the Cross: "I thirst." They are a reminder that all that she and her Sisters do for others is motivated by an ardent desire to satisfy the thirst of Christ for the salvation of the world!

In Summary

These four motives of love that produce joy in suffering are the result of the Holy Spirit's work in us. He enables us to appreciate and accept many purposes for suffering in God's plan, seeing its many fruits for ourselves personally as well as for many other people. Attempting to accept the Father's will even when it involves suffering, or trying to walk in Jesus' footsteps even when it follows the Way of the Cross, is not easy. But with the love provided by the Holy Spirit, it can still become a joy!

CHAPTER VIII

Our Lady, Cause of Our Joy

THE HOLY SPIRIT NO DOUBT inspired in Our Lady an over-whelming desire for the salvation of all those for whom Her Son, Jesus, died on the Cross. It is clear, even from the limited evidence we have in the Sacred Scriptures, that all through her earthly life Our Lady assisted Jesus in the work of our salvation and sanctification. This role, which she continues even now from Heaven, is actually twofold: maternal and exemplary. As Mother, she assists Jesus in a real though secondary capacity to obtain and distribute God's graces for all of us who are her spiritual children. As our example, she shows us in her very thoughts (= attitudes), words, and deeds how to correspond faithfully to God's graces.

Let us now look briefly at Our Lady's loving concern for souls as seen both in Sacred Scripture and in certain of her apparitions throughout the centuries.

OUR LADY'S ROLE IN SCRIPTURE

In Scripture we will focus on Our Lady both at Cana and at Pentecost.[1]

---

[1] We have already considered Our Lady's spiritual maternity as it is reflected both in the Annunciation at Nazareth and at Jesus' death on Calvary, as well as her spiritual joy at the Visitation.

CANA

At the wedding feast of Cana (John 2:1-11), Our Lady's role is linked with her great faith.

First of all, it moves Jesus to work His first miracle,[2] changing water into wine. When Our Lady initially makes her concern known to Jesus — "They have no more wine" — Our Lord's immediate response appears to be one of non-involvement:

> Woman, how does this concern of yours involve Me? My hour has not yet come (John 2:4).

Most people would probably have taken that response as a flat "no" to the request made, but Our Lady does not. She continues with unwavering confidence and trust that her Son will do something. This faith prompts her to give to the servants at the wedding feast an instruction filled with an evident expectancy that something would happen: "Do whatever He tells you." Moved by such trusting faith, Jesus manifests His power and glory, changing ordinary water into "choice wine."

A second effect, also traceable to Mary's faith, then happens. In a sense, it is even more significant than the physical miracle: Jesus' disciples came to have faith in Him:

> Jesus performed this first of His signs at Cana in Galilee. Thus did He reveal His glory, and His disciples believed in Him (John 2:11).

The faith of this first band of disciples is the beginning of the Church's faith in Jesus. Thus, the faith of the Church is influenced by the faith of Mary. Since faith is the beginning of discipleship (a person initially becomes a disciple by believing), Mary is rightly called the "Mother of the Church." She was the instrument of the Holy Spirit, helping to communicate life-giving faith to the first disciples of Jesus. What great joy there must have been at Cana!

---

[2] St. John in his Gospel refers to Jesus' miracles as "signs," because they reveal the deeper reality of Jesus' identity and the hidden purpose of His mission.

Our Lady continues to intercede for the Church in all its needs. She continues to be the Holy Spirit's instrument to bring others to spiritual life by inspiring in them a living faith in Christ, her Son. Thus, Mary's love prompts her to bring life to those who are to become brothers and sisters of her Divine Son, and her own spiritual sons and daughters!

PENTECOST

A second Scriptural example of Our Lady's concern for the salvation and sanctification of her spiritual children is her role of intercession at Pentecost. She herself already possessed the Holy Spirit in a certain fullness. This was so for two reasons. First, her privilege of being "full of grace" from the moment of her Immaculate Conception implies that she possessed the Holy Spirit, the Sanctifier, not only because He pours divine grace into our hearts, but also because He Himself is the supreme gift of grace given to us. Second, she possessed the Holy Spirit since He overshadowed her at the Annunciation, at the moment she conceived Jesus within her womb. The Incarnation was in a special way the work of the Holy Spirit in her. Our Lady would never have lost or even diminished her possession of the Holy Spirit, since she corresponded perfectly with God's grace throughout her entire life. God never leaves us; we would have to leave Him to lose His presence. Our Lady never left Him, not even in the slightest way.

Our Lady's presence at Pentecost was essentially one of intercession for the first disciples to receive the promised Holy Spirit. They formed the nucleus of the Church. St. Luke describes the setting as the disciples awaited the Holy Spirit's coming:

> They went to the upstairs room where they were staying: Peter and John and James and Andrew; Philip and Thomas, Bartholomew and Matthew; James son of Alphaeus; Simon, the Zealot party member, and Judas son of James.

> Together they devoted themselves to constant prayer.
> There were some women in their company, and Mary, the
> Mother of Jesus, and His brothers (Acts 1:13-14).

Her prayers assisted the disciples to dispose themselves to receive the promised Gift of God, the Holy Spirit, just as her faith had earlier assisted some of these very same disciples of her Son to have faith at the wedding feast of Cana.

These first disciples gathered around Our Lady in prayer in the Upper Room. Pentecost was truly the "birthday" of the Church. A new life in the Spirit was poured forth abundantly. Our Lady's role as "Mother of the Church" was clearly evident amidst the overwhelming joy of that holy day.

OUR LADY'S ROLE IN HER APPARITIONS

In a very real sense, Our Lady's maternal task of intercession has never ended, even now after her Assumption into Heaven. Throughout the centuries she has come as an ambassador of her Son, as a "dispenser" of His mercy to all her children. Let us cite but a few examples.

GUADALUPE, MEXICO

At Guadalupe in 1531, at a hill called Tepeyac, Our Lady appeared four times to a humble Aztec Indian named Juan Diego, and charged him with a special mission. He was to request of the bishop of Mexico City, Fray Juan Zumarraga, O.F.M., that a church be built at the site where she appeared. She wanted her children to come there and pray to her for all their needs. She said to Juan Diego:

> I am a compassionate Mother to you, to all your people,
> and to all others of my devoted children who will call on

me with confidence. Here I shall listen to the people's groans and sadness. Here I shall make well and heal their disappointments, their bitterness and pains. Listen and be assured of it in your heart; let nothing harm, trouble or disturb your countenance or your heart. Am I not here, I who am your Mother?

And come the people have, in endless numbers, throughout the centuries to pray with faith and fervor, seeking the compassionate intercession of Our Lady. In fact, as a result of her miraculous image on the mantle of now Blessed Juan Diego, nine million native Indians entered the Catholic Church in a ten year period. Even today, Our Lady of Guadalupe inspires countless numbers of Catholics, especially throughout the Americas.

PARIS, FRANCE

In 1830, Our Lady appeared twice to St. Catherine Laboure at the Motherhouse of the Daughters of Charity on the Rue du Bac in Paris. In her initial visit on July 18, 1830, Our Lady told the young religious that a prolonged period of suffering would come upon the whole world, but especially upon France:

> There will be an abundance of sorrows, and the danger will be great. . . The whole world will be in misery.

But Our Lady also held out a message of great hope and consolation. She promised in her motherly love that graces would be given, especially through prayer to her Divine Son in the Blessed Sacrament:

> Come to the foot of the altar. There great graces will be shed upon all, great and little, who ask for them. Graces will be especially shed upon those who ask for them.

Our Lady told St. Catherine that God had a mission for her. But that mission was not revealed until Our Lady's second apparition on November 27, 1830. Our Lady appeared in the convent chapel "in all her perfect beauty." She was seen holding a golden ball, surmounted by a small cross, lifting it up as if offering it to God. She told St. Catherine:

> This ball which you see represents the whole world, especially France, and each person in particular.

St. Catherine noticed that Our Lady's fingers were covered with rings set with precious gems; from some of these gems came brilliant streams of light while others had no rays. Our Lady explained:

> These rays symbolize the graces I shed upon those who ask for them. The gems from which rays do not fall are the graces for which souls forget to ask.

Finally, the appearance of Our Lady changed to that with which we are familiar from the Miraculous Medal. An oval frame formed around her, with the following words appearing in gold:

> O Mary, conceived without sin, pray for us who have recourse to Thee.

Our Lady then instructed St. Catherine:

> Have a Medal struck after this model. All who wear it will receive great graces. They should wear it around the neck. Graces will abound for persons who wear it with confidence.

This medal, originally called the "Medal of the Immaculate Conception" from the words framing Our Lady, was soon popularly called the "Miraculous Medal." This was due to the many great favors and graces obtained by those who wore it with confidence in Our Lady's intercession: conversions to the Catholic Faith, repentance of hardened sinners, faithfulness to God's will, peace in families, protection from harm, as well as countless cures and healings of all kinds.

Our Lady continues to obtain and bestow God's graces for her children, especially those who wear the Miraculous Medal as a sign of their love and devotion for the Mother of God.

LOURDES, FRANCE

On February 11, 1858, Our Lady began a series of eighteen appearances to a young girl destined to become St. Bernadette Soubirous. They occurred at a grotto along the banks of the river Gave in Lourdes. There the Blessed Mother, whom St. Bernadette described as the "Beautiful Lady," asked among other things that she pray for the conversion of sinners. This happened at the sixth apparition, on February 21st. A skeptical physician, Dr. Dozous, was present at this apparition. When he questioned young Bernadette about what happened, she gave him this explanation.

> The Lady stopped looking at me for a moment and turned her gaze far from me and above my head. Then she looked at me again and when I asked her why she was sad, she said to me: "Pray for poor sinners, pray for the world which is so disturbed." I was at once reassured by the expression of kindness and peace that I saw on her face. Soon afterward, she disappeared.

Our Lady, gravely concerned for the salvation of all her children throughout the world, requested prayers for the conversion of sinners. St. Bernadette responded generously and prayed unceasingly for sinners from that time on.

Our Lady's great compassion for her children moved her to

ask that a chapel be built at the site of the apparitions, so that people could come there in procession to seek her intercession. She especially wanted the sick to come. During one of her apparitions, Our Lady pointed out to St. Bernadette a mysterious spring of water; over the years it has brought healings and miraculous cures to countless of her suffering children.

Lourdes is truly a place of physical and spiritual renewal. It radiates the joy and peace of her who, in answer to St. Bernadette's question about who she was, called herself the "Immaculate Conception."

Fatima, Portugal

No apparitions of Our Lady convey her overwhelming care and solicitude for the salvation and sanctification of her children as do her appearances at Fatima in 1917. For six consecutive months, from May to October, Our Lady appeared to three young children, Lucia Santos and Francisco and Jacinta Marto, at a place called the Cova da Iria. The essential element of her message to the seers was a call to conversion of life and reparation for sin.

In the very first apparition, Our Lady asked the young children:

> Do you wish to offer yourselves to God in order to accept
> all the sufferings He wishes to send you, in reparation for
> sin and for the conversion of sinners?

With childlike simplicity and humility, they gave themselves completely to Our Lady's request. She assured them that God's grace would strengthen and protect them. This request highlights Our Lady of Fatima's call that all the faithful willingly share in the work of reparation for sins and intercession for sinners. She told the visionaries that many souls are lost from God precisely because there is no one to offer prayers and sacrifices for them.

At the apparition on July 13th, Our Lady allowed the children to see a vision of hell. Afterwards, she told the children:

You have seen hell where the souls of poor sinners go. To save them, God wishes to establish in the world devotion to my Immaculate Heart. If what I say to you is done, many souls will be saved and there will be peace.

Our Lady prophesied that World War I would end soon; however, she added that if people did not cease offending God, a worse war would begin by which God would chastise the world. She then gave the children her "peace plan" from Heaven:

To prevent this, I shall come to ask for the consecration of Russia to my Immaculate Heart and the Communion of reparation on the First Saturdays. If my requests are heard, Russia will be converted and there will be peace. If not, she will spread her errors throughout the entire world, provoking wars and persecution of the Church. The good will suffer martyrdom; the Holy Father will suffer much; different nations will be annihilated. But in the end my Immaculate Heart will triumph. The Holy Father will consecrate Russia to me, and it will be converted and some time of peace will be granted to humanity.

There can be no doubt of Our Lady's love and concern for our welfare, especially our eternal salvation. As the loss of souls from her Son brings sorrow to her Immaculate Heart, then their salvation must bring incomparable joy!

MARY, CAUSE OF OUR JOY!

In the Eastern Church, there is an ancient story that illustrates all of this well. According to it, when St. Andrew the Apostle died, he was met by his brother, St. Peter, at the gate of Heaven. St. Andrew asked him, "Peter, where is she?" He answered, "Andrew, she is not up here. She is down on earth, drying the tears from the eyes of all her children in the valley of tears!"

The Church reflects this in its prayers to Our Lady. Not only is Mary invoked in the traditional Litany of Loretto as the "Health of the Sick" and the "Comforter of the Afflicted," but also as the "Refuge of Sinners" and the "Cause of Our Joy." In the popular prayer, the "Memorare," the conviction of Our Lady's unfailing intercession is expressed in truly inspiring words:

> Remember, O most gracious Virgin Mary, that never was it known that anyone who fled to your protection, implored your help or sought your intercession was left unaided. Inspired by this confidence, I fly unto you, O Virgin of Virgins, my Mother.

The joy experienced by those who have received Our Lady's loving intercession can only be surpassed by the joy of Our Lady herself in giving it to us!

Our Lady's zeal for souls springs from her ineffable love for God and for all His people made in His image and likeness. They are children of the Father, friends beloved by her Son, and living temples of the Holy Spirit. Our Lady now loves each of them as her own child. Such love gave inexpressible joy to her heart, even in the midst of the great sufferings she endured with her Divine Son for the honor of the Holy Trinity and the salvation of the whole world.

Alongside her Son, Our Lady's twofold role as mother and model clearly shows her to be the most faithful instrument of the Holy Spirit in the divine plan of salvation. As the evidence of Sacred Scripture and her own apparitions reveal, her presence and intercession filled the followers of Jesus with the surpassing joy of knowing, loving and serving her Son. May she continue to be for us an instrument of the Comforter, the Spirit of Joy, in this life, until we come to possess the fulness of the Spirit's joy forever in the kingdom of Heaven!